D0378995

AN INTRODUCTION TO KANT'S ETHICS

This is the most up-to-date brief and accessible introduction to Kant's ethics available. It approaches the moral theory via the political philosophy, thus allowing the reader to appreciate why Kant argued that the legal structure for any civil society must have a moral basis. This approach also explains why Kant thought that our basic moral norms should serve as laws of conduct for everyone. The volume includes a detailed commentary on the *Foundations of the Metaphysics of Morals,* Kant's most widely studied work of moral philosophy.

The book complements the author's much more comprehensive and systematic study *Immanuel Kant's Moral Theory* (Cambridge, 1989), a volume that has received the highest critical praise. With its briefer compass and nontechnical style, this new introduction should help to disseminate the key elements of one of the great modern moral philosophies to an even wider readership.

An Introduction to Kant's Ethics

ROGER J. SULLIVAN
University of South Carolina

NATIONAL UNIVERSITY
LIBRARY   SAN DIEGO

CAMBRIDGE
UNIVERSITY PRESS

Published by the Press Syndicate of the University of Cambridge
The Pitt Building, Trumpington Street, Cambridge CB2 1RP
40 West 20th Street, New York, NY 10011-4211, USA
10 Stamford Road, Oakleigh, Melbourne 3166, Australia

© Cambridge University Press 1994

First published 1994

Printed in the United States of America

Library of Congress Cataloging-in-Publication Data
Sullivan, Roger J.
An introduction to Kant's ethics / Roger J. Sullivan.
p.   cm.
Includes bibliographical references.
ISBN 0-521-46208-8 (hard). – ISBN 0-521-46769-1 (pbk.)
1. Kant, Immanuel, 1724–1804 – Ethics.   I. Title.
B2799.E8S84   1994
170'.92 – dc20   93-40557
CIP

A catalog record for this book is available from the British Library.

ISBN 0-521-46208-8 hardback
ISBN 0-521-46769-1 paperback

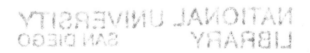
NATIONAL UNIVERSITY
SAN DIEGO
LIBRARY

CONTENTS

INTRODUCTION

UNDERSTANDING Immanuel Kant's moral theory can be a daunting task. Although Kant tried very hard to write clearly, even some of his contemporaries had difficulty figuring out what he was trying to say. In the following pages I have adopted a strategy that has not been commonly used by commentators but has proved extraordinarily helpful to my students in illuminating just those parts of Kant's moral theory that are usually the hardest for them to comprehend and appreciate.

Today we tend to approach the study of ethics from the point of view of the individual, with each person having her or his own special personal interests and relationships. Many of us, therefore, may feel more at home with a moral theory like that proposed by Sartre or Nietzsche, in which moral choices apparently cannot escape subjectivity; or with a moral theory like Aristotle's, which begins in the *Nicomachean Ethics* with the moral development of the individual person and the personal and private relationships of friends and family and only then, in the *Politics*, extends outward to the public order.

Kant's moral philosophy has also often been read (and with good reason) as concerned mainly with the moral character of individuals and of their actions. But if we approach it from that point of view, we may not have much sympathy for many of his claims, especially his insistence that our fundamental moral rules may override our personal concerns and cares. If, however, we begin with his political theory, we are better positioned to appreciate how his moral philosophy provides the underlying conceptual structure for a community life that can be shared by everyone. We can also understand better why he thought that the ultimate moral norm for us, even as individuals, should measure the fundamental policies on which we act for their suitability to serve as impersonal laws for everyone.

Great philosophy wrestles with perennial problems – problems that are not unique to any particular time or place but that arise again and again throughout history. So the fact that the political and moral problems Kant faced in eighteenth-century Prussia are strikingly similar to problems still occurring throughout the world confirms both his greatness as a philosopher and the enduring relevance and importance of his analyses to us today.

Since most people are introduced to Kant's ethical theory by reading his *Foundations of the Metaphysics of Morals,* references are given to that work, using the standard Academy pagination that almost all translations provide. Quotations from the *Foundations* are adapted from Lewis White Beck's translation (2d ed.; New York: Macmillan, 1990). The *Foundations,* however, does not contain Kant's entire moral theory, and we shall also discuss many doctrines that do not appear, or at least do not appear prominently, in that book. Readers may find the sources of those doctrines cited in the relevant sections of my *Immanuel Kant's Moral Theory* (Cambridge: Cambridge University Press, 1989).

1

A BEGINNING: KANT'S POLITICAL THEORY

IF we wish to learn Aristotle's ethical theory, we can turn to his famous *Nicomachean Ethics*. To learn the fundamentals of Utilitarianism, we can read John Stuart Mill's *Utilitarianism*. Students are usually introduced to Immanuel Kant's moral theory by reading his treatise with the strange title *Foundations* (sometimes translated as *Groundwork*) *of the Metaphysics of Morals*. Reading just this work can be misleading, however, for unlike Aristotle and Mill, Kant did not present his entire moral theory in a single book. The reason for this is that his philosophical system represented such a break with the past that it took him years to develop all its components.

If we wanted to learn everything he wrote about morality in his mature works, we would need to read his monumental *Critique of Pure Reason* (1781, revised in 1787), the *Foundations of the Metaphysics of Morals* (1785), his *Critique of Practical Reason* (1788), his *Critique of Judgment* (1790 and 1793), his *Religion within the Limits of Reason Alone* (1793), and his *Metaphysics of Morals* (1797) (for which the *Foundations* was an introduction), as well as *An Answer to the Question: "What Is Enlightenment?"* (1784), *On the Use of Teleological Principles in Philosophy* (1788), and *On the Proverb: That May Be True in Theory but Is of No Practical Use* (1793). During these same years he also published a number of other important works on, among other topics, politics and anthropology, such as *Idea for a Universal History from a Cosmopolitan Point of View, Speculative Beginning of Human History, What Is Orientation in Thinking?, The End of All Things, Perpetual Peace*, and *Anthropology from a Pragmatic Point of View*. This list does not include everything he wrote, but it gives an idea of what someone would need to read in order to master all the details of Kant's moral philosophy.

Clearly a person looking only for an introduction to Kant's moral theory cannot be expected to read all these, and that is why the *Foundations* is almost always the first and only book most students read. This still leaves us with the problem of avoiding misunderstandings, and trying to alleviate that difficulty is the purpose of this volume. The strategy used to minimize misunderstandings is to approach Kant's moral theory through his political theory. We will begin by discussing some of the issues that preoccupied him as he thought about morality.

Machiavelli. One challenge Kant had to face originated with Niccolò Machiavelli's infamous *The Prince,* written in 1513. Today much of Machiavelli's advice may seem to be simple good sense, for example, his insistence that even in peacetime a ruler needs a large and loyal military force. But he also claimed that because politics requires the effective use of power, when necessary a ruler may and should, for example, lie and break his word. The ruler "must be prepared to act immorally when this becomes necessary."

Machiavelli's claim "I have described things as they really are" was not particularly startling, for everyone knew that moral norms had been often ignored in political life. What made his claim special was the fact that no one before him had publicly *said* immorality might be acceptable, even obligatory.

Before him, philosophers had held that the center of human moral life lay within the circle of one's intimates – one's family and friends – so that moral enlightenment meant extending the standards of morality first to larger groups such as one's community, then to the state. Therefore, the same values held for a person both at home and in the public forum, and a good ruler was expected to be a moral paradigm for the people he ruled. But Machiavelli rent public life apart from private life. However, since people are always impressed by appearances, he also added that the prince needs to be concerned about how he is *perceived*. He needs to cultivate a *reputation* for compassion, good faith, integrity, and religious devotion.

Frederick the Great. The second set of problems was defined for Kant by the fact that he lived all his life under tyrants, most of it under Frederick the Great, who ruled Prussia from 1740 to 1786. While still a prince himself, Frederick studied Machiavelli's book, and with some encouragement from Voltaire, he even wrote a work "refuting" Machiavelli. (Voltaire believed that Machiavelli would have advised a prince-disciple to write a book publicly attacking him.) When he unexpectedly inherited the throne just as his book was being published, Frederick asked Voltaire to destroy all the copies of the book he could find!

As king, Frederick showed he had learned a good deal from his study of Machiavelli. He turned Prussia into a vast army camp that he supported by a program of economic development and taxation. He so enlarged Prussia by seizing neighboring land that today he is known as the founding father of modern Germany. Machiavelli would have smiled, had he been able to hear Frederick quoted as saying: "If there is anything to be gained by being honest, let us be honest. If it is necessary to deceive, let us deceive."

Life under Frederick was harsh. He regarded all those under him as his chattel, to be used as he liked. Publicly he held that the sovereign should be the "first servant" of the people; privately he had only contempt for what he called the "rabble." The nobles fared a little better than the peasants, but Frederick still allowed them only one choice of occupation: to serve as officers in his army.

Although Frederick's power was absolute, he still followed Machiavelli's advice about cultivating a reputation as a benevolent and tolerant ruler, a reputation that survives to this day. His biographers tell us that although he secretly despised the clergy, he cynically tolerated them because they preached the divine right of the king to the people's obedience. He also tolerated theological and philosophical controversies as long as the disputants still did what he ordered.

Kant never referred to Frederick's youthful foray into political philosophy.[1] When he did mention Frederick, he praised him as an enlightened ruler who allowed freedom of discussion, quoting him as saying, "*Argue* as much as you want and about what you want, *but obey!*" Kant's praise was not entirely misplaced, for Frederick William II, who ascended the throne in 1786, was far less tolerant of freedom of opinion than his father. Kant knew Frederick William's censors would be reading whatever he wrote,[2] and so he adopted an uncharacteristically self-deprecatory tone in his later political writings, suggesting at least to a superficial reader that his proposals (which could have been interpreted as treasonous) should not be taken seriously. He did this so successfully that even today the importance of his political writings is often not recognized.

The Enlightenment. Kant's intellectual world was also shaped by the Enlightenment, an intellectual movement promoted by profound advances of the "new" Newtonian science. Although Frederick had proclaimed himself a champion of the Enlightenment, it repudiated doctrinaire authoritarianism, whether political or religious. It put its faith instead in the power of reason, believing that reason would create a future of unending progress in the human condition. Kant's thinking was not only influenced by the Enlightenment; he was one of its leaders in Germany. As he later wrote, learning to make the decisions for oneself on the basis of one's own thinking is much more easily described than done, because it is so much easier to be lazy and let others do one's thinking for one. Renouncing a lifetime of "immature" dependence on authority and beginning instead to stand on one's own feet require a good deal of courage.

KANT'S LIFE

The relevant details of Kant's biography take little space. He was born in 1724 in Königsberg, the capital of East Prussia and one of Frederick's garrison towns. Kant knew what it was like to live as a peasant, since he came from peasant stock himself. (His father was a harness maker.) Because he showed such promise, Kant was able to attend a school called the Collegium Fredericianum, an institution run by Pietists. Pietism was an eighteenth-century fundamentalist movement within German Protestantism (similar to Methodism in the English-speaking world), to which Kant's parents also subscribed, that minimized the authority of the church and stressed individual moral conduct. He then attended the University of Königsberg, also staffed mainly by Pietists. The influence of this religious background is reflected in Kant's beliefs in the existence of God, in the dignity of each person, and in a universal moral code.

Kant spent most of his adult life on the faculty of the University of Königsberg. When he died in 1804, his countrymen flocked to his funeral, honoring him for the political ideals he had championed even while living under an absolute, militaristic monarchy, such as the equality of everyone before the law and the nobility of a just international peace. Today he remains one of the most influential philosophers of the "modern" period.

LIBERALISM

Kant's political writings have affinities with those of a group of writers whose philosophical thought underlies the fundamental documents of the American Republic. They included David

Hume and Adam Smith in Scotland, John Locke in England, Edmund Burke in Ireland, Friedrich Schiller and Wilhelm von Humboldt in Germany, Baron de Montesquieu and Alexis de Tocqueville in France, and James Madison, John Marshall, and Daniel Webster in what became the United States of America.

Common to these men was the conviction that absolutist governments, whether tyrannies or monarchies, intrude much too far into the citizens' lives: Ordinary people have no voice in determining their own destiny and no power to control that destiny if they have a voice. This criticism holds true not only for rulers with little or no concern for their people but also for paternalistic governments that benevolently but still despotically assume responsibility for the happiness of their citizens. Such states only exacerbate natural human tendencies to self-ishness and sloth, thereby encouraging dependence and ser-vility.

What people living in a totalitarian state lack above all is freedom, the freedom to pursue their lives and happiness as *they* see fit. According to liberalism, then, liberalism as opposed to the illiberality of tyranny, the proper function of government should be limited to protecting life and liberty.[3] This political philosophy, therefore, is committed to what is often called the "neutrality principle"; it recognizes that each person has the freedom, the capacity, and the responsibility to form his or her own conception of happiness and to seek that happiness, each in his or her own way, so long as this is done in a lawful fashion. Consequently, it is not the function of the state to try to balance the interests of different groups so as to promote the greatest happiness of the greatest number of its citizens. (That would later be the view of Utilitarians such as John Stuart Mill.) Rather, the role of civil laws conforming to that principle is to protect each person's freedom from interference by others. Laws are mainly concerned with happiness only insofar as they limit what anyone may do in its pursuit to the condition of allowing all others the same freedom to pursue their ideas of happiness.

In a series of essays that appeared throughout his career, Kant set out his proposals for a liberal state. John Gray has summed up the four main philosophical tenets underlying liberalism in his book with that title:

> 1. It is *individualistic,* in that it asserts the moral primacy of the person against the claims of any social collectivity.
> 2. It is *egalitarian,* inasmuch as it confers on all . . . the same moral status.
> 3. It is *universalist,* affirming the moral unity of the human species and according [only] a secondary importance to specific historic associations and cultural forms.
> 4. It is *meliorist* in its affirmation of the corrigibility and improvability of all social institutions and political arrangements.[4]

These four characteristics give us an admirable way in which to organize Kant's political theory.

THE RATIONALE FOR THE STATE

We can best approach Kant's political theory by asking: Why do we need a government at all? Why do we need laws? As Kant saw it, the most basic answer is: because people are always inclined to act egoistically, always wanting what is in their own interest, however that might affect others. History shows again and again that humans can and do act in the most reprehensible ways toward one another, treating each other merely as things, merely as a means of satisfying their own inclinations. For Kant, this lesson of history was reinforced by his religious background, for Pietism stressed the doctrine of Original Sin, with its emphasis on the dark, barbarous side of human nature. We all have what he called "an inextirpable propensity for evil": we all are tempted to pursue our own desires, whatever the cost to others. This is not a belief Kant was alone in holding. Although they did not all connect this view with religious doctrines as Kant did, most other political thinkers, both before and after him, agreed with his estimation of human nature and of the consequent need for civilizing political structures.

Like Thomas Hobbes, Kant recommended that we think of what life would be like in an "original state of nature," a lawless situation in which there would be no government and in which everyone could pursue his or her own desires without any constraints on how that might be done. The result? All would be at war with all, for everyone would be forced to live in a constant status of hostility toward and fear of others. Kant was well aware that states typically arise out of armed conflict, but he still suggested that, like Hobbes and Rousseau, we at least initially think of the state as if it had arisen out of a social contract with its citizens. If people actually had once lived in a state of nature, they would finally have been motivated, if only out of fear of even more awful evils, to leave this condition of constant conflict and enter into a social contract for a society that could protect their lives and their property as well as provide a peaceful tribunal for resolving disputes.

True to the liberal tradition, then, Kant regarded the fundamental task of government as negative, as imposing those constraints that are necessary to protect and promote each person's freedom. The legal system of the state must constrain both the power of the sovereign and the citizens' unregenerate desires in order to establish the conditions under which people can live together in peace as a community. The basic laws of the legal code therefore should set out negative obligations, *duties* prohibiting people from interfering with the freedom of their fellow citizens. (Few terms have more importance than "duty" in Kant's political theory, and, as we shall see, in his ethical theory as well.)

For Kant, then, the most basic function of civil law is not to grant entitlements but to lay down obligations. Whatever the benefits arising from living in the state, Kant believed that citizenship should be construed as a *task,* a responsibility to contribute to those moral conditions necessary if political security and order are to endure and flourish. By contrast, rights are derivative: they arise only from corresponding duties that the state enforces.

THE UNIVERSAL PRINCIPLE OF JUSTICE

Hobbes had argued that people will yield the freedom they possess in the state of nature to civil authority only if they believe it is in their best personal interest to do so. He therefore held that the justification for any state must be egoistic in nature. He further held that the state will have the power necessary to constrain the universal tendency to selfish and unruly behavior only if the power and authority of the sovereign, whom he compared to a leviathan, a "mortal god," are absolute.

But Kant argued that the overriding characteristic of a good state is, as Aristotle had also thought, justice, and clearly justice is not guaranteed merely by the fact of absolute governmental power. He therefore held that, whatever might originally motivate people to submit to civil authority, the ultimate *justification* for a society of free citizens must be *moral* in nature. Since moral convictions are so often based on different and conflicting religious or other cultural norms, how might it be possible to generate a system of laws that would be morally acceptable to everyone?

Kant's solution was to propose a prepolitical principle of legislation, based on reason alone, that he called the "Universal Principle of Justice."[5] This principle, which has the role of regulating the entire formal legal structure of society, states that only those civil arrangements are just (or right) that allow the most freedom for everyone alike. Stated as an imperative for the citizens, it commands: "Behave in such a way that your choices are compatible with the greatest amount of external freedom for everyone."

Such a principle may not seem to be a very promising basis for a just social union, but it in fact turns out to be surprisingly powerful. Because it underlies all the laws of the state, it requires that the essential legal structure protect the maximum freedom of all the citizens to pursue their own happiness and well-being by limiting lawful actions to those to which all members of a state can consent. It therefore is the antithesis of tyranny, in which the "rightness" of civil laws is dictated by sheer power and the people are subject to the arbitrary whims of whoever happens to possess that power. It also provides a foundation for the obligation of the people to live in a law-abiding fashion. As we shall see, the Universal Principle of Justice in an enriched form is also the fundamental moral norm for our personal life as well.

Finally, since this principle is the basis for any morally acceptable code, Kant maintained that it should be recognized and respected by every political body and in every political system. What can ultimately validate the universal binding force of this principle? Not the church, which too often had tyrannically supported the status quo or at least had not protested it. Not the king, who had too often promoted his own desires by claiming to have the divine right to be the voice of God in earthly matters. Not the feelings and self-interest of the people, because in the case of conflicts between people with different feelings and interests, the only resolution would be through force; and if force is the ultimate validation of civil authority, Hobbes's view would prevail, not Kant's.

Given the foundational character of this principle as well as his commitment to the Enlightenment, Kant held there can only be one ground for the Universal Principle of Justice: the authority of reason alone, as evidenced in the moral thinking of ordinary people. They are all bound by moral obligations, and they therefore must innately possess a fundamentally correct understanding of morality and its norms (404).[6] The ability to think for oneself, to determine for oneself what is morally right and morally wrong, is, he wrote, "inherent" in everyone by virtue of the human capacity for reasoning. What we find by an appeal to reason, he continued, is that the denial of the principle generates an absurdity: "Any action that clashes with everyone's freedom is just." *That* would be a prescription for civil chaos rather than a principle constraining just such civil chaos. The appeal to the authority of reason alone, actually an appeal to the principle of noncontradiction, therefore proves the correctness of the Universal Principle that laws of justice must be principles to which everyone can rationally assent, whatever other moral beliefs they might have.

There is a certain circularity here, since it is the power of moral reason that underlies its own law. This is not invidious, however, for basing morality on anything outside itself would destroy morality.

A SYSTEM OF LAWS

To summarize, then, as Kant saw it, a state can be based either on force, on the arbitrary desires of a despot, or on the rule of law, itself based on respect for every citizen and on the rational ability of each person to be self-governing, to make decisions and take responsibility for himself or herself. Civic duties are fundamentally negative rules of cooperation, limiting how people may behave toward each other. Underlying the legal structure of such a state must be the Universal Principle of Justice, which requires that civil laws ban conduct that would make communal collaboration impossible and which insists

13

that the most basic laws are those each person can agree to and obey.

Like the Universal Principle of Justice, substantive laws immediately derived from it must be recognizable a priori – that is, as Kant put it, by reason alone. Since they are laws that ordinary people are obligated to obey, they must be laws that everyone of average intelligence can recognize as right and binding on them. Such fundamental laws forbid any behavior that would infringe on the person of others, on their status of equality, on their ability to be self-determining and to function responsibly and with dignity, or on anything to which they have title, such as property, as well as legislating the obligation of parents to care for their children. Taken together, these subsidiary principles make up a system of what Kant called the laws of natural justice.[7]

Because of the generality of such principles, there is a need for further, more definite legislation, what Kant called "positive laws," having the force of law only after being enacted, to make matters of right more definite. Positive laws specify what is required in matters that are otherwise arbitrary, pertaining, for example, to rules of the road and to procedures for acquiring and transferring property. They may vary from place to place and take into account, for example, local customs, cultural beliefs, and economic factors, but they should not conflict with the Universal Principle of Justice. Since the state has both the right and the duty to enact such laws, obedience to them should also be recognized as a civic duty and, from the point of view of ethics, as a moral obligation as well.

Few actual states will enact a system of laws that does not fail in one way or another to promote justice. In such cases, changes must be made, Kant wrote, but "not immediately or impetuously," only gradually and prudently so as not to deny the plebiscite the respect due it.

THE DIGNITY OF THE INDIVIDUAL

We can now understand how, first and foremost, liberalism is committed to recognizing the dignity and worth of each and every human person. This concept may seem obviously right to us today; we find statements of it in such fundamental documents as the Bill of Rights and the Charter of the United Nations as well as in Martin Luther King's "Letter from a Birmingham Jail." But at the time Kant was writing, it was a deeply radical proposal, opposed both to the then most prevalent kind of government, tyranny, as well as to the traditional conviction that what confers dignity on a person is only one's social position and rank – being royalty or nobility. To the contrary, Kant argued, what gives *every* person dignity is neither social status nor special talents nor accomplishments but the innate power of reason, the capacity of each individual to think and choose, not only to shape his or her own life but also to protect and promote reciprocal respect by enacting laws that can form the legal structure of life for everyone (438, 440). Kant called this power and responsibility to act on the Universal Principle of Justice "autonomy." In Kant's liberal political theory, the power of autonomy is what gives every person moral authority and status against the might of the state.

It is important to emphasize that the basis for autonomy does not lie in each person's feelings. Because desires are contingent and vary so much from person to person and even during each person's life, they cannot be a stable and reliable basis for universal rules of conduct able to sustain the fabric of society (442). In fact, according to Kant, appealing for practical guidance to anything that lies outside a person's reason, whatever it might be, is the very antithesis of autonomy, that is, heteronomy (441–3). The institutions of society must be regulated by laws based on reason; only they will consistently protect freedom and ensure justice.

The notion of reciprocal respect underlies two further, co-ordinate principles of liberalism: equality and universality.

EQUALITY

To be just, the liberal state must also be *egalitarian* in the sense of recognizing that everyone has the same innate moral status. Recognizing that everyone has the ability to be autonomous means that the fundamental laws of the state should apply to everyone equally, with no exceptions made in favor of the wealthy or the powerful, the gifted or the educated. There should be no legally privileged class nor should there be any special protected interests. Likewise, there should be no legally underprivileged class, for no one has the civil (or moral) right to use others *merely* for his or her own purposes. Rather, everyone is entitled to equal respect before the law.

According to Kant, civil egalitarianism does not mean the government must try to ensure equality in possessions and power that can be gained by a combination of talent, industry, and luck, any more than it should penalize those who happen to be physically or mentally superior in order to achieve what today is often referred to as "an even playing field." As he saw it, the promotion of economic egalitarianism is, first of all, unworkable, because everyone has different and conflicting interests and aims; what is more important, the effort to achieve economic equality would also require continual violations of justice and civil liberty. What political egalitarianism does require is equality of opportunity in the sense that everyone must be permitted to strive for and, if possible, attain whatever status to which he or she aspires within the opportunities of a free society; and no one may unlawfully hinder others' aspirations.

UNIVERSALITY

The principle of equality also implies a principle of universality. Since justice demands a juridical condition that protects each person's freedom by protecting everyone's freedom, the administration of justice must be impersonal: it may not discriminate between persons on the basis of contingent particularities, including whatever special needs and interests different individuals may happen to have. The statue of Justice symbolically wears a blindfold because the law should apply to everyone alike, without regard for race, religion, sex, or national origin. As Gray puts it, the liberal state is *"universalist,* affirming the moral unity of the human species and according [only] a secondary importance to specific historic associations and cultural forms."

This characteristic runs directly contrary to a popular view today, the claim that cultural pluralism is more fundamental and more important than the moral unity of society as a whole. According to this view, the special interests of the various national and ethnic and religious groups making up the state should all be given special privileges in the public forum. But Kant in effect argued that regarding cultural diversity as primary would imperil the very existence of the state, for that would violate the demand of justice that the most fundamental civil laws of society be genuinely *universal,* applying to everyone alike. From this follows an equally important corollary: to hold universally, such laws also must bind *absolutely.* If they do not, Kant maintained, they will soon be turned into generalities, with all sorts of exceptions made for particular individuals or groups who believe they are deserving of special exceptions and advantages under the law.

REPUBLICANISM AND THE GENERAL WILL

In a tyranny, the ultimate authority behind the law is supplied by sheer coercive power. Kant regarded the Universal Principle of Justice as providing the only alternative to the tyrannical exercise of power: the authority of government rests with the rational consent of the governed. He therefore concluded that the ideal government must be a republic, in which the people obey laws they together could have legislated through their representatives. Such a government may have any of three forms of sovereignty – monarchy, aristocracy, or democracy – as long as the constitution is republican at least in spirit. Only a government that is republican in spirit will respect all its citizens as free, equal, and autonomous individuals and will restrict civil law to universal negative principles of justice and will enact positive laws compatible with such principles, laws therefore that could be chosen by every autonomous person. Only a liberal republic will protect life and property and ensure an environment of reciprocal respect within which each person can lawfully pursue whatever activities he or she wishes, unimpeded by others.

What will keep a representative government from degenerating into a democratic tyranny that ignores the rights of minorities is the requirement that the executive and judicial branches be constitutionally insulated from direct popular pressures that could reintroduce arbitrary privileges on behalf of the majority at the expense of a minority – or vice versa. The legislative authority, however, should remain with the people, who represent "the general will" or "the united will of the people," expressions Kant borrowed from Rousseau.

These expressions should not be taken as referring to the actual preferences of the citizens, for it is just such self-serving desires that, by focusing on private or special interests, tend to promote favoritism and to subvert the passage of just and impartial laws. Nor did his adoption of these expressions mean that Kant thought that the enactment of laws requires an actual popular unanimity of the citizenry. Even within a civil society, people remain in an "ethical state of nature," so often concerned only with their own desires that empirical unanimity is not a genuine possibility. The will to which Kant was referring is the Universal Principle of Justice, present in the rational will of every citizen, in contrast to the "particular will," which is based on each person's special interests. This is a norm that obligates the legislature to attend to questions of justice by asking, not whether any proposed piece of legislation will agree with the popular will of the electorate, but whether it could arise rationally out of a contractual agreement with the people: Can the people rationally consent to this law and rationally impose it on themselves, no matter what the cost? Such a question concerns the public and common good, not the private and particular good, and guarantees justice, for each chooses for all.

Kant also connected the Universal Principle of Justice with the notion of the general will by means of what he called the "Principle of Publicity." This principle does not insist that every policy a ruler adopts must be stated publicly (Kant recognized that diplomatic negotiations often need to be carried out in a confidential manner). Rather, since laws still need to conform to the general will even when they have been enacted by someone other than the citizens, the Principle of Publicity functions essentially as a negative test of the moral acceptability of laws not enacted by the people: any maxim of a legislator is unjust if publicly stating it would arouse such universal opposition as to frustrate its purpose. (As we shall see, this test is a version of the Categorical Imperative, which, in matters of justice, rejects any maxim proposed by an individual that cannot be stated also as a law for everyone without generating a contradiction and, in that sense, arousing universal opposition.)

Kant wrote that, given the selfishness typical of human nature, we "cannot count on" everyone always to respect the person and property of others (438). So the state may and often must use coercion to counteract such abuses. It might seem that any use of force would be incompatible with republican ideals, but Kant believed that the legitimacy of using coercion to protect freedom can be shown to be just by an appeal to the ultimate norm of rationality, the principle of noncontradiction. It is self-evident, he held, that whatever "counteracts the hindering of an effect promotes this effect and is consistent with it"; and so force used to protect freedom is consistent with everyone's harmonious exercise of freedom of behavior. This, Kant thought, is the only coercion that may be exercised against the citizens by the state.

HOPE AND A LEAGUE OF NATIONS

Many Enlightenment thinkers believed in the inevitable historical progress of the human race, but the actual historical record gave Kant (and still gives us) little reason to think that the moral character of the human species will ever change substantially for the better. Because he was acutely aware of what seemed to him to be a universal propensity for people to prefer evil to good, Kant believed that people cannot be relied upon to contribute to progress toward civil justice out of moral motives. But he also thought this tendency was not totally unredeemed, for those same egoistic and antisocial impulses that motivate people to compete for superiority over each other can bring about progress as an unintended consequence, so that the human species will still, if erratically, "make continual progress toward the better." What counts here as "better" is not universal happiness and contentment (the government in George Orwell's *1984* later embraced that goal) but laws that conform more closely to the Universal Principle of Justice and conditions that are more conducive to a life in which the dignity of persons can be defended and promoted.

Kant's view here reflects the final characteristic of liberalism – its *meliorism*. Liberalism was, and is, a fundamentally hopeful political philosophy that holds that, even if we take a somewhat negative view of human nature and despite the wrongs that occur in the course of time, justice and peace will prevail. (The enormous evils committed since the Enlightenment do not seem to support such optimism.)

Kant's political philosophy was not limited to discussions of the internal affairs of individual states, for he believed that the highest political good requires global peace secured by just agreements between states. In his most famous political essay, *Perpetual Peace,* he described states as "moral persons" with the same obligations toward each other as any other persons. Like individuals living apart from a juridical condition, states also initially exist in an international, lawless state of nature, always actually at war or continually preparing for war, and they, too, tend to resist yielding their power to another political body. But once again Kant relied on motives of self-interest, rather than on moral motivation, to promote international stability and peace.

He believed that the same self-interest that could drive individuals from the state of nature to a juridical society will drive nations toward an international federation, a league of nations in the form of a worldwide republic of sovereign powers. Once that is accomplished, mutual economic dependence will keep them there, and the unsocial, now nationalistic desire to surpass others will induce countries to promote the education of their own citizens so they can compete more effectively with other nations. Ironically enough, Kant wrote, materialism and avarice, social exploitation and stratification, all may be "indispensable means to the still further development of human culture" and then of moral consciousness, leading to international law securing the rights of all the states.

KANT'S MORAL THEORY

Before examining Kant's moral theory in detail, we need to summarize the ways in which his political liberalism captured the main themes of his moral theory. We will begin by setting out what Kant learned from the philosophical descendants of Machiavelli.

First, moral norms cannot be based on experience. What experience shows is that people have engaged in all sorts of conduct; and appealing to experience simply destroys the possibility of constructing a moral point of view. In both the preface to the *Foundations* (387–91) and the first pages of its second section (406–12), Kant focused on the need for a "pure moral philosophy completely cleansed of anything empirical."

Second, it is crucial to situate morality firmly within the public forum. There it consists fundamentally in standards of justice prohibiting policies others cannot rationally accept and therefore articulating norms fit to serve as laws within a state that respects all its citizens. As a consequence, in the *Foundations* Kant's first formulation of the Categorical Imperative, the Formula of Universal Law, requires us to test proposed basic moral maxims by the criterion of whether they can serve as public laws for everyone (413, 421).

Third, necessity is never an adequate excuse for violating moral standards, for they hold universally and absolutely. It hardly seems an accident that in the *Foundations* Kant used the Formula of Universal Law to test just those policies Machiavelli had proposed – of lying and of making lying promises – for their moral acceptability (e.g., 402–3, 422).

Finally, effectiveness is not a measure of moral character, for, as Machiavelli had seen, effectiveness can be used to justify immorality. It is no accident, then, that in the *Foundations* Kant emphasized that effectiveness is a prudential – an amoral, rather than a moral – norm; it is not a test for identifying the "good will" (394–6, 415).

What did Kant learn from the Enlightenment? He learned that the basis for the dignity of each person, and so the most fundamental authority for each person's life, is her or his own reason. Each has the power of autonomy and therefore the right and the responsibility to be self-governing, in control of his or her own destiny insofar as that is possible. Consequently, each person's dignity is inalienable and limits the rightful exercise of power by both the state and the church. This doctrine appears most dramatically in the *Foundations* in the second formula of the Categorical Imperative, the Formula of Respect for the Dignity of Persons.

What did Kant learn from Frederick the Great and his son? He learned that tyranny wrongly treats its citizens as mere things, some to be favored, others not, but all to be used only to serve the ruler's desires. The first formula of the Categorical Imperative therefore insists that just laws must apply to everyone without exception. Those laws are, originally at least, negations, not imposed simply to use people but legislated to protect everyone's freedom. As we shall see, the second formula also insists that no one be treated merely as a means to achieve someone else's aims.

THE RELATION BETWEEN PUBLIC AND PRIVATE MORALITY

Surveying Kant's political theory has served to introduce us to the fundamental Universal Principle of Justice, the moral basis for a just civil union. That principle, stated in the form of what, in the *Foundations*, Kant called the Categorical Imperative, is also the fundamental ethical norm for each individual's personal, private life – that is, what one does alone or to, with, or for others in the privacy of the home and in one's private associations. In neither our civic nor our private life, for example, may we violate the respect owed others. There therefore can be no notion of a "private morality" in the sense of a kind of morality *competing with* public morality. In fact, it would be precisely the decision to make one's inclinations exempt from public morality and supreme in one's life that would make a person morally reprehensible. Within the Kantian view, private morality in the sense of egoistic, antisocial self-centeredness means

23

a decision to live in an ethical state of nature – lawlessly, outside the fundamental strictures of morality.

Because both are based on the Universal Principle of Justice, Kant held that although we need to *distinguish* between the public and private aspects of human life, they should not be *separated*. He was convinced, in fact, that personal morality cannot exist and flourish except within the context of civil society. Through its laws, the state promotes morality by realizing some moral ends such as freedom, thereby creating an environment within which moral living can flourish. However, even though public laws of justice extend to the whole of human moral life, such laws cannot fully encompass all that life, which also includes considerations of character as well as special personal relationships. That is why Kant did differentiate carefully between morality in the public and private realms.

He did so in the following way. The original Universal Principle of Justice and the domain of civil law are restricted to *actions* that affect others: what is essential to good public order is only correct behavior. So what Kant called the "doctrine of law" concerns *only* our "duties of outer freedom," or "juridical obligations." Civil authority can use coercion to enforce its laws, but it cannot and does not try to legislate or enforce whatever reasons and purposes citizens may have for obeying its laws. It may, for example, constrain the citizens from violating the respect due others, but it cannot insist that they do so *because* they respect them. (This is the limited truth in the saying that we cannot legislate morality.) For that reason the enforcement of mandatory civic duties does not officially appeal to moral motives but rests only on penalties for violations, prudential incentives that presumably everyone, even those lacking a strong moral character, will want to avoid.

The personal domain, by contrast, is much richer, for it includes the internal forum, that is, moral character, which is defined by internal law-giving. A person of good moral character is one who not only does what is right but does so from the specifically ethical motive of dutifulness: because it is the dutiful thing to do. (Thus, the notion of "duty" has even more prominence in Kant's ethical thought than in his political theory.) Because all such duties are subject only to *self*-legislation and *self*-constraint, Kant called them "duties of inner freedom."

Finally, our personal ethical life also extends beyond mainly negative and universal moral duties to include significant positive and particular obligations. That is why Kant entitled the discussion of these duties "the doctrine of ethics."[8] We will discuss these matters further in the following chapters.

NOTES

1. Kant seemed to make a point of never mentioning Machiavelli's name in his published writings. In his essay *Perpetual Peace,* for example, he criticized any ruler using the Machiavellian excuse of necessity to justify using whatever devious practices might promote his own private advantage, but he identified such a person only as "the supposedly politically practical man." He also deleted a reference to Machiavelli from the subtitle of a draft of his *Theory and Practice,* leaving only "Against Hobbes."

2. It may have been for similar reasons that Kant adopted the head-of-state immunity doctrine, which views the state and its leader as indivisible, so that an attack on the leader must be regarded as directed also at the state. Kant argued that there can be no right to forceful civil resistance to unjust laws nor any right of the people to depose or punish a ruler for unjust actions. On the one hand (as we shall see in Chapter 8), Kant thought that personal moral reformation requires a revolution in moral character; but on the other, he held that civil reformation should come about only gradually, by evolutionary reform, in order to avoid a reversion to the lawless state of nature.

3. Classical liberalism as depicted here is now generally referred to as "conservativism," in contrast to the "revisionist" liberalism held, for example, by Jeremy Bentham and John Stuart Mill and underlying President Franklin Roosevelt's New Deal. The latter kind of liberalism, mainly based on a Utilitarian type of justification, champions state interventionist policies typical of the modern welfare state, which assumes direct responsibility for the citizens' well-

being and happiness. By contrast, Kant's kind of liberalism aimed to limit the functions of the state to the promotion of justice and the protection of freedom. However, Kant did not deny that the state must have *some* concern for the welfare of citizens when they are unable to provide for their own most basic needs. Although he considered this primarily an ethical duty of human beings to help other human beings in need, he also allowed that when people enter into a contract with the state, the state does assume an obligation at least to keep them alive along with the right to tax the more wealthy to help do so. History seems to indicate that the positive role of government cannot be limited as severely as Kant argued.

4. John Gray, *Liberalism* (Minneapolis: University of Minnesota Press, 1986), x.

5. This norm is more usually translated as "the Universal Principle of Right" (*Recht* in the original German). Today, however, people tend to use the term "right" to canonize whatever it is that they wish to do. Kant had quite a different meaning for the word: to say that a person has a right is to say that that person has a legally enforceable claim against others within the context of civil law. The term "justice" rather than "right" is therefore less subject to misinterpretation by contemporary readers.

6. All numbers in parentheses refer to the standard Academy pagination for the *Foundations of the Metaphysics of Morals,* to be found in nearly all translations. References to Kant's other writings can be found in the relevant sections of my *Immanuel Kant's Moral Theory* (Cambridge: Cambridge University Press, 1989).

7. Kant's critics frequently have argued that Kant's moral–political theory faces a serious problem when it tries to determine which maxims or laws are morally acceptable and which are morally unacceptable, for the same behavior can instantiate different and sometimes conflicting maxims, that is, conflicting policies stating general rules of conduct. This objection has much more strength if we approach morality from the viewpoint only of the individual than if, like Kant, we think of the test of moral acceptability as asking whether maxims might serve as laws of conduct within the public context of a community of free, equal persons. Then it is easier to see that the *point* in rejecting certain maxims is that they cannot coexist as part of a system of laws that recognizes the dignity of each person.

As we shall see, even in the private sphere Kant's theory requires us to judge whether maxims could hold within an ethical society with negative nonjuridical laws, forbidding us to harm others, that extend beyond but are still modeled after those of the public sector (they hold universally and absolutely). In that realm, our motivation plays a critical role in influencing how we act and in determining our moral worth; but our moral obligations to *others* are not dependent on (our judging) their moral worth or lack of it. As we shall also see, we have significant discretion in how we carry out our positive duties.

8. At times Kant contrasted the terms "moral" and "ethical," the former applying to juridical duties and the latter to nonjuridical matters. But he also used the term "moral" to include both juridical and ethical duties; in the *Foundations,* for example, he wrote that the motivation behind an action determines its "moral worth" or "moral content." From here on, therefore, the term "moral" will usually be used to include the ethical.

2

THE CATEGORICAL IMPERATIVE: THE ULTIMATE NORM OF MORALITY

W E are now ready to examine Kant's doctrine in his famous little book with the off-putting title of *Foundations* [or *Groundwork*] *of the Metaphysics of Morals*. In the preface to that book, he wrote that he intended mainly to set out the ultimate moral norm and defend its ability to obligate us (392). We have already seen that law in the form of the Universal Principle of Justice, but in the *Foundations* Kant restated it so it would apply not only to our behavior but also to our aims and motives.

We have also seen that in Kant's political theory the relations between persons in the state of nature and even within civil society are marked by discord arising out of conflicting desires. This strife has its counterpart within each individual, in our experience of internal moral conflict between our reason and our desires. We may not *want* to obey the moral law; we may also have – in fact, often have – desires we would prefer to satisfy. For this reason, *all* moral laws appear to us as imperatives. Moreover, because nothing can justify disregarding our moral obligations, they obligate us absolutely, or categorically. Consequently, in the *Foundations* Kant called the ultimate moral norm the "Categorical Imperative."[1]

There is and can be but one such ultimate norm (421), but Kant offered three different versions or formulas, each with its own particular emphasis. He preferred the first for its formality, but he also thought that alternative ways of wording it might make its meaning more transparent and compelling to us, his readers (436–7).

Formula 1 – the **Formula of Autonomy** or of Universal Law: "I ought never to act in such a way that I could not also will that my maxim should be a universal law" (402).

Formula 2 – the **Formula of Respect for the Dignity of Persons:** "Act so that you treat humanity, whether in your own person or in that of any other, always as an end and never as a means only" (429).

Formula 3 – the **Formula of Legislation for a Moral Community:** "All maxims that proceed from our own making of law ought to harmonize with a possible kingdom of ends as a kingdom of nature" (436).

Once we understand how the Categorical Imperative functions as our ultimate moral norm, Kant believed that using it should not involve any special difficulty. After all, he wrote, the moral law commands everyone's obedience, so everyone should be able to use it (403–4). We commonly face two problems in our moral life: deciding what are the right moral policies and having the moral strength to observe them. Today we might debate which is the harder task, but Kant was convinced that it was the cultivation of a sufficiently good character. "What duty is," he wrote, "is plain of itself to everyone," even to those of the "commonest intelligence."

THE FIRST SECTION OF THE *FOUNDATIONS*

In his political writings Kant found the source of the Principle of Justice in the general will, that is, in the authority of reason common to everyone. In the first section of the *Foundations* he likewise aimed to support the Categorical Imperative by appealing to the reasoning of ordinary people (394, 397). If we attend to how people determine their general moral rules, he wrote, we will see that the Categorical Imperative is, in fact, the moral norm good people use (402). His strategy in that first section, therefore, was to analyze what he took to be our ordinary notion of good moral character, that is, what it means for a person to have a "good will."

Kant began his analysis with the claim that nothing is superior to morally good character; it alone is always and unconditionally good. He supported this claim by pointing out that everything else we consider good – physical and mental health and economic resources – can be used immorally. Even happiness can tempt a person to act in a morally careless way, and, besides, he continued, we do not think that a person who leads an immoral life is deserving of happiness (393).

He then in effect asked three questions, and he called his answers to these questions his "propositions."[2]

The first question was, What makes a person morally good (have "a good will")? In his answer (394–6), Kant pointed out, first, that when we act, we always act to accomplish something; every action has some goal or other. Yet we do not consider people to be morally wanting when, despite their best efforts, they fail to achieve their goal. If the goodness of moral character does not depend on the good things a person is able to accomplish, it must then depend completely on a person's intentions. The one thing we *always* can do is to form our intentions as we ought, and in that sense the categories of "success" and "failure" are not relevant to the quality of a person's moral character. These, of course, are not the intentions that, according to the old saying, pave the road to hell, for they are not merely idle wishes but, as Kant wrote, involve a striving with all one's might, showing that one's intentions are genuine. Morally good character is therefore intrinsically good, that is, good in itself, just for what it is and not good merely insofar as it is effective in achieving something further (394).

The next question was, What kind of intention makes a person morally good? In his answer Kant introduced an important distinction between two radically different kinds of motives: the desire for happiness and the motive of dutifulness, that is, of doing what we morally *ought* to do *because* it is what we ought to do. Having a morally good intention must mean acting from the motive of duty (the claim some commentators have taken to be his first proposition). To support this contention Kant again turned to the judgment of ordinary people. In their judgment, he wrote, there is a radical difference between being happy and being morally good; people do not think that the fact that someone seeks or achieves happiness means that person also seeks or achieves moral goodness, or vice versa (442). What this means, then, is that if our desires happen to lead us to do the morally right thing, that does *not* indicate we have a morally good character (397–8).[3]

We might respond to Kant by arguing that a morally good intention is one that promotes morally permissible happiness. But in that case also morally good character still must depend on intending to do what one should, and the only morally good intention is the intention always to do (to act on the maxim or policy to do) one's duty (397, 399–400).

Kant was not alone in insisting that we need to do the morally right thing with the right intention. Aristotle, for example, had held that, to be good, a person should be motivated to act rightly by the recognition that it is right or "noble" to do so. But Kant's view of the human condition was deeply influenced by his study of the innumerable atrocities committed throughout history as well as by his Christian background, and he placed much more emphasis than Aristotle on how often we all are tempted to act wrongly.

The term "right," he concluded, does not acknowledge how our wants clamor for satisfaction so that we typically experience morality as a *constraint* on our desires, mandating what we *should* do, independently of what we may or may not *want* (397, 400, 420n). Because we seem never to be completely free of the propensity to pursue pleasure rather than virtue, it is therefore not accurate to refer to what is morally required of us simply as "what is *right*," nor to describe moral motivation only as the disposition to do what is "morally *right*." Morality always appears to us in what elsewhere he called the "dry and earnest" form of *duty*, our obligation, what we ought or ought not to do (397, 412–13, 434, 449).[4] No moral philosopher before Kant had placed so much emphasis on the notion of duty, and few ideas have greater prominence in his theory. In this regard he continues to exercise a profound influence on both the vocabulary and thought of moral philosophers.

That answer gives rise to the third question: What does it mean for a person to intend to act "from duty"? And the answer is: to resolve to do whatever the moral law obligates one to do, out of respect for that law (400). Kant introduced the notion of respect here to emphasize that the ultimate moral motivational force is not a desire to satisfy our wants but having such a regard for moral requirements as to be willing, if it is necessary, to frustrate any and all desires we may have. Again, the only motive of specifically moral quality consists of a law-abiding disposition of respect for and submissive obedience to the Categorical Imperative, often in the face of opposition from desires and inclinations (400, 439). Since dutifulness or conscientiousness abstracts from any ends we may desire, it requires us to comply with the moral law out of respect for it, regardless of any desires we may have and regardless of anything further we may or may not achieve.

Having gone through this analysis of morally good character, Kant finally asked, What is this moral law that can give rise to such respect as to outweigh every other motive? Since it is not a rule for satisfying our desires, it must be a rule for satisfying only the requirements of our reason. Likewise, since it is not a rule for effectively achieving some goal or "matter" like happiness, it must be a rule with an intrinsic characteristic: that *any* person could and would adopt it who acted on the basis of reason rather than desires (401, 421, 431).

Kant then stated the overriding norm as: "I ought never to act in such a way that I could not also will that my maxim should be a universal law" (402). This, as we have seen, is the first formula of the Categorical Imperative, which underlies all the moral judgments of ordinary people (403). It appears to us as an imperative because we can disobey it and it commands us to act in a law-abiding fashion, first, by adopting maxims or policies that can serve as moral rules for everyone and, second, by conscientiously acting on those maxims ourselves.

As Kant used the term in both his second and third answers, "maxims" are practical rules that enunciate a person's intentions (400n). In the *Foundations,* however, he unfortunately did not discuss how maxims can be of varying generality. In order to understand how the Categorical Imperative operates as our moral norm, it will be helpful to draw a parallel now between his moral and his political theories. (Kant often described the formulation and adoption of moral maxims as a kind of legislation, not unlike the enactment of public laws.)

Like the Universal Principle of Justice, which judges the rightness of civil laws, the Categorical Imperative is a purely formal and therefore universal norm for the moral acceptability of possible policies. Such policies, like the laws of natural justice in the public forum, have substantive content, for they refer to general kinds of actions that any agent, including those with generally described positions or roles, may (or may not) or must (or must not) do in certain generally described kinds of situations. They are the sort of policies or principles that underlie our more immediate and particular "surface" intentions.

We have seen that the laws of the civil order conforming to the Universal Principle of Justice are objective; that is, they are rules that can be accepted and acted on by everyone. Likewise, if our fundamental maxims conform to the Categorical Imperative, they too enunciate policies or principles that are objective and can hold for everyone. By contrast, Kant called maxims "subjective" that hold only for one person or subject and that may be based on that person's ignorance or desires (420n). Subjective maxims, however, can be raised to the level of objectivity, even though they take into account special features

33

such as time, place, and personal relationships, as long as they conform to the norm of objectivity, the Categorical Imperative (400n, 420n).

THE SECOND SECTION OF THE *FOUNDATIONS*

Despite his confidence in the moral reasoning of ordinary people, Kant also was aware that the claims of "ordinary moral awareness," to use his expression, may be confused, incomplete, and even misleading. And so, in the second section of the *Foundations,* after devoting several pages to the argument that we should not try to base morality on experience (406–12), he developed another way to explain the origin and nature of the ultimate moral rule.

Just as desires cannot provide a secure basis for universal laws of a just state, so also they cannot be the basis for objective principles of our personal ethical life. To be an objective norm, the Categorical Imperative, like the Principle of Justice, must be based on reason alone (it must have what Kant called a "pure a priori foundation"). If that is so, we should be able to arrive at the moral law just by analyzing the Idea of a "rational being as such," that is, a perfectly rational agent (412–14, 426). (Since morality is based on reason alone, then such an agent would also necessarily be perfectly moral or "holy.")

Although we have no experience with a perfectly rational being, Kant thought that such a being obviously would have to be one who always thought rationally. What is the minimal requirement for rationality? Although Kant did not discuss this explicitly in the *Foundations,* the ultimate law underlying all coherent thinking is the logical, and so completely formal, principle of noncontradiction. That principle sets out a universal, if primarily negative, requirement for *every* use of reason: two contradictory judgments cannot be both true or both false; if one is true, the other must be false. Likewise, a self-contradictory statement is meaningless. Insofar as one thinks coherently, then, one necessarily observes the principle of consistency; one does not make claims that are self-contradictory or that contradict one another. This principle is an objective law, holding true for a perfectly rational being like God, "the supreme intelligence," as well as for all other rational beings.

Theoretical thinking involves assenting to or withholding assent from judgments about what *is* the case, while practical thinking involves deliberations and decisions about what *ought* to be the case (387). So the meaning of "contradictory" needs to be adjusted appropriately when used within the context of practice: A perfectly rational (or holy) *agent* is one who never *wills* in violation of the fundamental principle of reason, the principle of noncontradiction; such an agent necessarily adopts and acts on only maxims that are both self-consistent and consistent with one another (412–13, 422–4). Because this principle is also an objective law, one holding for every rational agent, it may be expanded to read: Insofar as any agent acts on reason alone, that agent adopts and acts only on self-consistent maxims that will not conflict with other maxims any such agent could adopt. Such maxims can also be adopted by and acted on by all other agents acting on reason alone.

Kant called this principle the Law of Autonomy, and since it rests on an analysis of the notion of a purely rational/moral agent, it is an analytically true description of such an agent (437, 445). This is shown by the fact that its denial results in a practical absurdity: a purely rational agent is one who adopts and acts on self-contradictory (i.e., rationally incoherent) maxims. So the ultimate moral law turns out to be a practical application of the logical principle of noncontradiction. We also saw this in Kant's defense of the Principle of Justice: to deny that principle results in a practical incoherency. A morally good person is therefore one who does not act except in ways in which every other good person may act.

Applied to human agents, who can recognize the obligatory nature of the moral law but are affected by sensuous desires and can still choose to act contrary to it, that law must be stated as an imperative (412–13). Then it is equivalent to the first formula of the Categorical Imperative, the Formula of Autonomy or of Universal Law, at which Kant had already arrived by analyzing our ordinary notion of good moral character (437).[5] In the form of an imperative, it reads: "Act on maxims that you can also will be made laws that hold universally."

THE DUAL ROLE OF THE CATEGORICAL IMPERATIVE

To avoid any possible confusion here, we need to be clear about the fact that the moral law has two different functions: to command our obedience and to test possible maxims.

The first function. Because we are not holy, we can always elect to act immorally, and so the ethically required thing to do always appears to us not just as right but as obligatory, our *duty*, and the moral law appears to us as the Categorical Imperative. Since it is our own reason that mandates the obligatory Law of Autonomy, Kant argued, we cannot evade the prescriptivity of that law, no matter how inclined we may be to do so. The moral law is still present in our rational awareness, commanding our obedience, without any regard for our desires and inclinations. It inevitably condemns us if we violate it. This is also why, Kant wrote, we first become aware of the moral law in the form of a prohibition, and why he frequently described morality as a limitation on our desires and inclinations. This, then, is the first function of the Categorical Imperative: to obligate us to obey it.

The second function. The Categorical Imperative also functions as the test of the moral quality of possible maxims. As we have seen, since its role is to identify practical rules that can serve as policies for everyone, the maxims to be tested must be stated in very general terms.

To be our ultimate moral norm, the Categorical Imperative

must tell us not only what is morally wrong but also what is morally permissible and what is morally obligatory (439). To do that, it must be both the necessary and the sufficient condition for judging the acceptability of a possible maxim. So we need to ask whether it is analytically true that a completely rational agent could act on the maxim under consideration. As we have seen, a completely rational agent acts only on maxims that are both self-consistent and consistent with one another. To test maxims of conduct, then, we need to ask, Is this a maxim that a purely rational agent can adopt? Or alternatively, could this maxim function as a law for a community of rational agents legislating not only for themselves but for all other such agents as well? This kind of test might be outlined this way:

I. *Major Premise:*   The Categorical Imperative.
    Minor Premise: The proposed maxim or policy.
    Conclusion: A substantive moral principle in the form
                       of a categorical imperative.

Note that this kind of deliberation concludes not in actions but in *maxims:* practical principles or policies. This is the kind of decision procedure involved in Kant's four examples in the *Foundations.* We will discuss such judgments in more detail in the next two chapters.

One question may still linger. Why is it morally unacceptable to adopt a maxim that violates only a *logical* norm? Kant's answer is that logic always takes on the interest of the activity in which it is used (459n). When used in moral reasoning, then, the principle of noncontradiction does not remain *simply* a logical norm. Instead, it becomes the ultimate standard of both a just political life and a morally good personal life.

THE ROLE OF MORAL JUDGMENT

Once the Categorical Imperative has helped us determine what general policies or maxims we should adopt for our lives, we still need to make more-specific moral judgments about how to act here and now (389, 404). Because Kant was not concerned with this kind of judgment in the *Foundations*, he does not discuss them explicitly, and many readers confuse the first and second kinds of judgment. This second kind of judgment, schematized somewhat artificially and simplistically in a syllogism, goes as follows:

II. *Major Premise* (a substantive universal moral principle): Making false promises is a morally wrong practice.

Minor Premise (particular moral facts): This action is a case of making false promise, and I am not the kind of person who makes false promises. (We identify the maxim of a proposed action as one we have already rejected as immoral.)

Conclusion: Therefore, I will not do this action. (Kant called this the "subjective determination of the will.")

To understand the place of this kind of judgment in our moral life, it may be helpful to set out again some relevant parallels between Kant's accounts of political and ethical legislation. As we have seen, both the Principle of Justice and the Categorical Imperative function as purely formal norms for the legislation of substantive maxims or policies – in one case for civil legislation and in the other for ethical legislation. In both cases, the rightness of such policies or principles can be recognized in what Kant called an a priori way, by reason alone, for their denial generates a practical contradiction. Kant did not claim to offer a complete canon of such policies, but the maxims he did provide seem to indicate that if they are stated with sufficient generality, their number need not be large in order to encompass most of our ordinary moral decisions.

The public order then requires more-specific, positive laws that still must conform to those general principles. Likewise, because Kant thought of acting rationally as acting on a rule, he believed that in our personal life each of us must choose more specific maxims on which to act. These are the sorts of maxims in which the reasoning that is schematized in II concludes. If these maxims lay out moral obligations, they are maxims on which everyone else in a similar situation should act. If they set out actions that are morally permissible, then they are maxims that all others similarly situated could adopt and act upon. Naturally, the more specific maxims become so as to include both circumstantial details and the motive of an agent, the narrower is the range of those who could also rationally adopt them. Within the parameters of the general policies, the question becomes, Could anyone in my particular situation find it reasonable to act this way?

In the volume for which the *Foundations* is the introduction, his *Metaphysics of Morals*, Kant held that different kinds of moral judgment need to be learned in different ways. To learn policies, he suggested that students work out a sort of moral catechism containing the kinds of basic moral maxims discussed in his book. He then proposed that the students sharpen their ability to make particular moral judgments by applying those policies to various scenarios; and he offered some twenty cases as exercises for discussion.[6]

Different situations present us with different kinds of problems. We always must decide whether any general policy is relevant to the situation in which we find ourselves, and if so which. Occasionally we may have special difficulty relating a given policy to a complicated and perhaps ambiguous situation. Sometimes we may also be faced with what Kant called "conflicting grounds of obligation," in which we feel torn between apparently incompatible obligations.[7] Other times we may also be concerned about how the passage of time may affect our moral responsibilities.

Because such decisions cannot be completely formalized into a set of directives, Kant did not try to offer a single decision procedure. He did point out that sometimes we can understand new situations by comparing them to other, more familiar situations. Since he held reason to be a faculty of rules, he also thought that other times our reflections can be stated as a series of maxims of increasing specificity, concluding in judgments about how to act.

But even in the latter cases, there is no formal procedure to be observed, since the manner in which we should take into account all the details of our individual situations cannot be laid out ahead of time. Simply having morally acceptable policies does not by itself determine for us what may or may not be morally relevant or important in each instance. The ability we need is a kind of native endowment, Kant thought, like eyesight, that he called "mother-wit." But he also thought we can develop skill in making such judgments through practice, by experience, whether personal or vicarious (through casuistry). Through simply living, facing ordinary moral problems day by day, we all accumulate a store of moral experience to help us judge how to act; we all develop some sensitivity to the features to which we should attend. Moreover, most of the situations in which we find ourselves are familiar ones, and we do not need to deliberate over how to act. We simply act on maxims that reflect our long-standing commitments and values.

The fact that he did not offer any more specific advice about how to make our more particular judgments is not a defect in Kant's theory. No moral theory can offer more. As Aristotle had seen centuries earlier, practical or moral reason is a critical faculty, a creative faculty, and an imperative faculty. As a critical faculty, it can construct policies and rules on which to act and *that* is the limit of moral philosophy proper and of its rules as well. As a creative faculty, it must bridge the cognitive distance between principles and actions, and that is the role of judgment (389). As an imperative faculty, it causes our deliberations to issue in actions, and that is the role of moral character.

But despite having a limited role, moral theories in general and Kant's in particular can still offer us a great deal of clarity we might otherwise lack about our own moral life, thereby empowering us to improve its quality. In the following chapters we will see in more detail how Kant's theory can do so.

EMPIRICAL CONTENT

The ultimate moral norm is a purely formal law, completely empty of all content, like a statement-form written in logical notation, again showing its roots in the logical principle of non-contradiction. In order to apply it to the human condition, then, we have to supply a context of empirical information. So in the preface to the *Foundations* Kant described moral philosophy as having "an empirical part" – what he called "practical anthropology" (387–8).

As Kant saw it, such information concerns only things that are commonplace and readily accessible to everyone of ordinary intelligence. We need to know, for example, that we are dependent physical beings with needs to be met with the help of our reason; that we are emotional as well as rational beings; and that we can and do experience conflict between our emotional and our moral interests. We also need to know the ordinary causal laws of the world in which we live, and we need to be acquainted with everyday social practices and how they are carried out.

The fact that the application of the Categorical Imperative requires us to take into account features about human beings that we can learn only from experience does not mean that our moral life is therefore based upon experience or anthropology. Our moral judgments still must be grounded on the ultimate Law of Autonomy, given by reason alone.[8]

MISUSING THE CATEGORICAL IMPERATIVE

By now it should be clear that the Categorical Imperative plays only a background role in our everyday moral life.[9] On the basis of having already faced and resolved many moral problems, we generally already have on hand a coherent set of moral maxims or policies adequate to guide our everyday decisions, like the principles Kant set out in the *Foundations*. But because Kant did not explicitly distinguish in that work between judgments about general maxims and judgments about specific decisions, many readers have been led to think that we should use the Categorical Imperative in all our everyday decisions. They have been misled into thinking that Kant claimed that our immediate moral decisions must look something like this:

III. *Major Premise:* The Categorical Imperative.

Minor Premise: The maxim of a possible action, for example, I want to try to become a philosophy teacher (or whatever).

Conclusion: Therefore, I should not try to become a philosophy teacher (or anything else, nor should anyone else!).

The implied reasoning process is this: If we were to apply the Categorical Imperative directly to this case and ask whether the maxim in question could also be a universal law for everyone, we should have to conclude that no one should try to teach philosophy, for then there would be no one to tend to all the other things that need doing, there would not be enough teaching jobs available, and so on. It is clear that using the Categorical Imperative in this fashion ends in an absurdity – an indefinitely large number of conclusions ruling out virtually every proposed action.

What has gone wrong in Syllogism III is a confusion between the kind of deliberation appropriate only to testing very general maxims for their moral acceptability (Syllogism I) and the kind of deliberation appropriate to our immediate decisions about how to act (Syllogism II). Moreover, in this case the reasoning rests not on the notion of volitional consistency but on an evaluation of empirical consequences, that is, on prudential criteria; and the result is that we generate only absurdities.

NOTES

1. As Kant used it there, the term "categorical," like the term "hypothetical," referred to the manner in which an imperative binds an agent (414–16). A categorical imperative declares an action obligatory without any reference to anything further, whereas a hypothetical imperative states that an action is necessary to attain something else a person wants or may want. So "categorical" here should not be interpreted merely as a remark about grammatical form, namely, that a moral imperative has no explicit condition, although that is also often the case.
2. Kant failed to designate which is his first proposition, so different commentators identify that proposition differently.
3. In the example of a grocer who treats his customers honestly (397), Kant distinguished between morally correct ("legal") actions done from an immediate desire and such actions done in a more calculated way as part of a long-range program of self-interest. He contended that we have more difficulty in identifying the specifically nonmoral or prudential quality of the motivation in the first kind of action because, although all actions motivated by desires are only instrumentally good, those motivated by an immediate inclination more closely resemble actions motivated by duty, which causes us to take an immediate interest in an action as good in itself. (It may be added that on the basis of the information he gives, Kant's presumption that the grocer acted out of self-interest lacks support.)
4. Kant also referred to all the actions, the maxims of actions, and the ends commanded by the Categorical Imperative as our "duties." (See, e.g., 429, 454.) There are, as we would expect, various such duties, such as fidelity to contracts, beneficence, honesty, and so on.
5. The Law of Autonomy would never appear as an *imperative* to a perfectly rational being like God, for the very nature of such a being is always and necessarily to act on that law (414, 434, 439).

 In the *Foundations* Kant occasionally clouded the difference between the Law of Autonomy as a principle analytically elucidating the concept of a perfectly rational (or holy) agent and that same principle as an imperative obligating us, given that we are imperfectly rational human agents. As a consequence, his claims in 440 and 447 that the principle of morality is *not* analytically true can certainly seem perplexing.

Because Kant stressed that the Categorical Imperative is a "synthetic a priori proposition," it may be helpful to touch on this topic. In the analytic proposition, "A perfectly moral agent always acts on the Law of Autonomy," the predicate ("always acts on the Law of Autonomy") makes explicit only (at least part of) the meaning of the subject ("a perfectly moral agent"). We can reach the predicate-concept by analyzing the subject-concept, and that is just what Kant did in the second section of the *Foundations*.

By contrast, that analytic statement becomes a synthetic a priori proposition when restated as a principle for contingently moral agents like us: "A contingently rational/moral agent *should* be an agent who never acts on maxims that violate the Law of Autonomy." The subject-concept is an agent who may or may not obey the Law of Autonomy; and the predicate-concept (one who never acts on maxims that violate that law) is not contained analytically in the notion of the subject. This is a synthetic principle because it joins or synthesizes two different ideas. Moreover, the two concepts are joined with a "should" that can be justified only in an a priori fashion, that is, by reason alone.

The principle of noncontradiction acts as both the necessary and the sufficient condition of truth for *analytic* judgments, which, if they are true, are necessarily so. For such claims the principle of noncontradiction determines both what cannot be true and what must be true. Consequently, when we test maxims by the practical version of that principle, we need to state them as analytic sentences and simply ignore the fact, as irrelevant to this task, that the Categorical Imperative and all substantive moral principles must appear to us as synthetic a priori propositions.

6. When constructing his cases, Kant usually presented a conflict between morality and happiness in the most dramatically vivid way possible; choosing one meant renouncing the other. He did this because he believed the greatest danger to the purity of morality occurs just in those situations in which we apparently can accomplish the greatest imaginable benefits by moral compromise. In all such cases he would have condemned making moral decisions on the basis of consequential considerations.

7. See the section Conflicts between Moral Rules in Chapter 6.

8. In the *Foundations* Kant overemphasized the "purity" of moral phi-

losophy for human beings: his explanation there of a good will applies only to sensuous and imperfectly rational human agents; and the concept of duty as rational self-constraint is a "mixed" concept, formed of both rational (or a priori) and empirical elements and applying only to contingently rational agents like us.

9. The role of the Categorical Imperative in Kant's theory can be compared to that of the Greatest Happiness Principle in Rule-Utilitarianism: both should be used only to generate policies, expressible in maxims or administrative principles, that then can help guide our everyday decisions.

3

THE FORMULA OF AUTONOMY OR OF UNIVERSAL LAW

AS our ultimate norm of practical consistency, the Categorical Imperative obligates us to adopt and act only on policies that can also serve as objective laws because they are self-consistent as well as consistent with other such policies: "Act only according to that maxim by which you can at the same time will that it should become a universal law" (421). It is therefore appropriate to give the first formula the title the "Formula of Universal Law." Like the Universal Principle of Justice, this formula is a negative test of possible or actual maxims of happiness. We may not claim to be exempt from obligations to which we hold others, nor may we claim, on the basis of our own special interests, permissions we are unwilling to extend to all others. The requirement of universality, therefore, is a criterion of reciprocity: what is forbidden to one is forbidden to all; what is permissible for one is permissible for all; and what is obligatory for one is equally obligatory for everyone else. Hence we must judge maxims in a *disinterested* fashion, particularly in those cases in which we happen to have the greatest interest.

But whereas the Principle of Justice focuses on behaviors to be constrained by civil authority, this formula adds the *ethical* requirement that if we are to act as moral agents, we must ourselves freely will the universality and reciprocity the moral law commands. The actual formulation of moral maxims may originate with others; we each do not have to begin everything anew, as if no one before us had ever understood anything about morality. But since the only kind of constraint con-

46

sistent with the freedom necessary for autonomy is self-determination, our adoption of moral maxims must be based on our recognition of our obligations both to obey the moral law and to exclude any determining influence outside our own reason, whether that be the will of another or our own desires to gain pleasure or avoid pain. That this claim is analytically true is shown by the fact that its denial results in the self-contradictory claim that freedom can be compelled. Since only such self-legislation is autonomous, this version of the Categorical Imperative may also be called the "Formula of Autonomy."

AUTONOMY: PRACTICAL LAWFULNESS

Kant offered several versions of the first formula that explicitly state how to use it as the procedural norm for moral legislation: "Maxims must be chosen as though they should hold as universal laws of nature" (436; see 421). Testing maxims for their suitability to serve as laws for everyone presumes that we are clear about what makes a law a law. It would not do for Kant to take the Prussian policies of privilege as his model of law, because they exhibited just the sort of arbitrariness he wished to rule out of morality. So he turned to a long philosophical tradition and recommended that we think of the laws of nature as a model for the laws governing the moral world.[1] Such laws, "in their form" (i.e., as laws), hold universally: they do not discriminate between individuals they bind, and they are exceptionless (431).

We therefore can test the moral status of proposed maxims by asking whether they can fit together as laws to constitute the framework for a world of freedom in the manner in which physical laws govern the world of nature. This, Kant wrote, is an exercise of our understanding, not of our imagination, for we are testing our proposed legislation, not by its imagined possible empirical consequences, but by its logical consequences, using the logical norm of consistency already present in the reason of the members of the moral world.

Such a world – a moral world – is only an Idea of reason; it is only an ideal, a possibility. What is real is the unconditional requirement of reason that our proposed policies could serve as laws in a moral world of which we ourselves would also be a part. In its first formula, therefore, the Categorical Imperative forbids us to act on maxims that either cannot *also* be *conceived of* as laws without contradiction *or* are incompatible with other lawful maxims and so cannot be *willed* as laws without generating contradictions. If a maxim cannot pass both tests, it is not fit to serve as a practical law in a possible moral world.[2]

If we attend to the way in which ordinary people make their moral judgments, Kant wrote, we will find that this is just the way they do so. When morally challenging a particular way of acting, people typically ask: "What if everyone acted that way? Would I be willing to live in a world in which everyone acted like that?"

TESTING THE MAXIM OF A LYING PROMISE

Let us now examine in a more concrete way how Kant thought the Categorical Imperative functions as a practical principle of noncontradiction. Using this norm cannot be so difficult that only a professional logician would be competent to apply it – not, at least, if Kant was right in claiming that ordinary people can and do use it with astonishing ease. To see how all this works out, let us examine his discussion of a lying promise. The question at issue, he wrote, is: "May I not, when I am in distress, make a promise with the intention not to keep it?" (402).

Before going farther, it is worth pointing out that all Kant's examples in the *Foundations* mention the agent's aim in acting on a particular maxim. In the case of the lying promise, it is to get out of financial difficulty; in other cases, it is to avoid further physical and psychological distress, to devote oneself to a life of pleasure, or simply to avoid some inconvenience. All the maxims being tested are maxims of happiness, with the underlying aim of satisfying some desire.

In his political theory, as we saw, Kant regarded the main task of the state as constraining our tendency to pursue our own interests without regard for the cost to others. Similarly, in his moral theory he held that maxims of self-interest are just what need to be checked for their moral acceptability. We typically question the moral acceptability of a maxim only when we already want something the maxim will help us get. Even though "the moral worth of an action does not lie in the effect which is expected from it" (401), the Categorical Imperative will reject the maxim of a proposed policy if it is teleologically self-contradictory, that is, if the point of the maxim is incompatible with that maxim stated as a universal policy or if it is incompatible with other policies we already know we are morally obligated to follow.

To see just how the Categorical Imperative functions as a *practical* principle of noncontradiction, it will be helpful to do a quick review. In modern propositional logic the principle of noncontradiction is usually stated as $\sim(p \cdot \sim p)$; that is, "it is not the case that both p and not-p." Within the moral context of choosing maxims, a practical contradiction consists in maintaining both that a maxim or rule should hold universally and also that it "subjectively should not hold universally but should admit of exceptions" (424). In terms of the Aristotelian logical "Square of Opposition," which Kant of course knew, the opposition is either between O (particular negative) and A (universal positive) judgments, or between I (particular positive) and E (universal negative) judgments. It is not rational to try to will contradictories, since they are mutually exclusive.

Let us now look at Kant's example. Let us symbolize a person's policy, such as, "I will make lying promises when I am in need and when it is advantageous to do so," as m^i (with m standing for "maxim" and i for "individual"). We cannot test this maxim just by itself. This is exactly why Kant held that the Categorical Imperative requires us to "Act only on that maxim through which you can *at the same time* will that it should become a universal law," or, put negatively, "Never choose except in such a way that the maxims of the choice are [*also*] present as universal law in the same volition" (421 and 440). To test the original maxim, then, we must also state it as a universal law, or what Kant called "a law of nature," which we will symbolize as m^u (with m standing for "maxim" and u for "universal"). We then join it with the individual's maxim to form the conjunction $(m^i \cdot m^u)$. The Categorical Imperative then requires us to determine whether this conjunction, $(m^i \cdot m^u)$, is in fact a contradiction.

In the case of Kant's example of a lying promise, we now have the following conjunction:

> I intend to make lying promises whenever it is advantageous to me to do so, and at the same time I also will a world in which everyone else will make lying promises, even to me, whenever it is advantageous for him or her to do so.

Clearly, we need to have commonplace knowledge of what the practice of promise making is all about. To make a promise is to engage in verbal behavior consisting in giving one's word to perform some future action, and to accept a promise means believing that the other person is telling the truth and will fulfill that promise. Kant simply presumed that we all are aware that, in the absence of any other moral considerations, this is a morally permissible social practice. There clearly is no conflict between a person's intention to engage in the practice of making and keeping promises and being willing that everyone else also do so.

As only a little reflection shows, however, it is not rationally possible for the individual's maxim of lying promising to coexist with that same maxim as a universal law of conduct. The logical consequence of that conjunction is that no performance could count as "making a promise."[3] The practice of promise making would then disappear, along with all practices that depend on promises (403, 422). Because lying promises are parasitic on the practice of promise making, we also could no longer make lying promises. As Kant wrote, we therefore cannot even *think* of a universal law of lying promises, for such a law would be self-contradictory and in effect self-defeating (424). The test does not of itself imply that we must make promises but it does tell us that if and when we do, we may not make lying promises.[4]

Kant pointed out how this example indicates that morally wrong choices typically are characterized by a contradiction in our will: the adoption of two different standards of conduct, one for ourselves and another for others. In the case of the lying promise, we expect others to follow *their* appropriate role in the interaction, namely, to believe we will keep our promise; and at the same time, although we engage in promise-making behavior, we also intend from the start not to keep our promise. We will that the standard for promising hold for us only as a general rule, with exceptions in our own favor.

It cannot be stressed too strongly that although the Categorical Imperative requires us to assess the consequences of the adoption of a particular maxim, it is concerned only with the *formal* or *logical* consequences. Our choosing to act in a certain way does not have the *empirical* consequence of causing everyone to act in the same way; we obviously do not have such power. Nor, as John Stuart Mill later claimed, is the Categorical Imperative a test of the *desirability* of the consequences or of the unity of those consequences under the title of happiness. If empirical consequences are irrelevant, obviously any interest we might have in such consequences is also of no moral importance.

CONSISTENCY WITH OTHER MAXIMS

A maxim that fails the first test of consistency is thereby shown to be contrary to duty and so is morally forbidden. But if the Categorical Imperative is to function as both our necessary and our sufficient moral norm, it must also be able to identify our positive moral obligations, at least in very general terms. But positive maxims that ordinary people judge to be morally unacceptable do not necessarily generate contradictions in conjunction with themselves stated as universal laws.

Kant had this problem in mind in his fourth example, in the second section of the *Foundations*. Here, a person whose life is flourishing adopts the maxim of simply ignoring everyone else (423). He will neither contribute to nor detract from their welfare, and he is willing to have everyone else treat him in exactly the same fashion. Such a maxim would not be inconsistent with itself as a universal law. "It is possible that a universal law of nature could subsist in harmony with this maxim," Kant wrote. "If such an attitude were a universal law of nature, mankind could get on perfectly well," certainly better than in an ethical state of nature, in which people mistreat each other. But Kant still denied that it is possible for us to will rationally that such a principle hold as a law. (To "will" such a law is not the same as to *want* such a law. Given his view of human psychology, Kant suspected that in such cases we often would prefer to have others help us without our also being obligated to help others.)

We need to apply the first formula in a somewhat different fashion to test maxims concerning our positive duties. We have seen that the laws of a moral world must be mutually consistent. Similarly, there must be practical consistency both within each person's moral life and between the lives of all others inhabiting that world. Neither can consist of an incoherent and lawless concatenation of conflicting laws. So a maxim is morally unacceptable if, when made a law, it contradicts another law or other laws that we must adopt because they are morally obligatory (423–4).

Let us return now to Kant's fourth example. When making decisions about our relationships with others, we obviously must take into account the fact that all human beings are dependent and vulnerable, with needs that constantly have to be met. It also is clearly rational for us to will the means to goals we may have. When everything is going well and our needs all are met, we may abjure dependence on others. But we know that there will come times in the future when, because we are not by nature self-sufficient, we all will have to rely on others. We all will need the help of others to promote our natural welfare and happiness, which we cannot totally renounce and which we may have an indirect duty to cultivate. We all also need others to help us fulfill our direct moral obligations to develop and sustain ourselves as rational agents with non–self-sufficient natures, for example, by caring for our health and enhancing our abilities through education. We therefore cannot reasonably make the universal claim that everyone can always remain independent of everyone else's beneficence. Eventually we all would have to contradict the maxim under examination by having to ask for the help of others. We therefore cannot will that a maxim of never helping anyone be acceptable as a permissive law for rational agents like us (423).[5] We are required, rather, to adopt the maxim "to help others where we can" (398; see 430).

In this way, the Formula of Universal Law can and does generate positive as well as negative obligations – here the obligation to help others. Positive duties have special features that we will need to examine later. For example, we enjoy a good deal of discretionary room when deciding exactly whom to help, how much, and when. This is why Kant describes positive duties as "wide": a decision not to act on the maxim of helping others in any particular instance is not necessarily an exception to or a violation of that general maxim. This is a matter for judgments that need to take into account whatever contingent factors have moral weight in the situations in which we find ourselves.

When we tested the policy of making lying promises, we saw that such a maxim results in what may be called a teleological contradiction: its adoption is inconsistent with the given end of promising. This presupposes that the maxim concerns an action that is an instance of a general practice, like promising, with objective teleological criteria against which to measure the maxim under consideration. But all sorts of actions do not have some "given," uncontroversial "point" to them against which to test relevant maxims. For such cases, Kant maintained that we must *construct* a system of ends (or "matter") that should be regarded as obligatory for everyone (see 427–8). We have seen that moral requirements necessarily appear to us as obligatory; likewise, these ends must appear to us as obligatory, for they must be regarded as good even when contrary to our inclinations. We have both the right and the duty to identify some ends as obligatory, he argued, for we would be unable to obey the Categorical Imperative if we could not know what it requires of us. Without some such ends, we could rationally assess many actions only insofar as they might be instrumentally good for obtaining things we desire, and that would make all our relevant policies only hypothetical and cause great areas of our lives to have no discernible moral worth.

When identifying these ends we need to regard ourselves from two different viewpoints: simply as moral agents and also as embodied moral agents with finite and dependent natures. Each viewpoint, or interpretation, of human existence leads to its own kind of morally obligatory ends.

In the first case, Kant argued, all moral agents or persons are morally obligatory ends; and since the only persons with whom we are acquainted are human beings, we must regard human beings (or "humanity") as having intrinsic, moral value.[6] The value of persons then sets limits both on our intentions and on our actions. Because we have a duty to live up to our own moral worth, we are obligated to avoid both attitudes and actions incompatible with our own dignity or that of others, such as lying, avarice, and servility. When we examine the second formula in the next chapter, we will explore these duties in more detail.

In the second case, a substantive moral theory for human beings must take into account that we are moral agents who are also physical and dependent beings. Kant held that here our most fundamental personal obligatory ends are self-preservation and the cultivation of our mental and physical powers.[7] Caring for our physical and mental well-being enhances our capacity to get and enjoy what we want. We may recognize such well-being as a natural good that we should value just on the basis of self-love, of concern for our own welfare. But the *moral* ground for developing and sustaining our abilities is not regard for any advantage that gives us. As Aristotle had pointed out, all our powers and skills are capacities for moral opposites; they all can be used for either morally good or morally bad purposes. Regardless of any prudential advantages they offer, then, our moral reasoning identifies natural goods and rational ideals as morally obligatory only insofar as they are necessary for maintaining, enhancing, and exercising our moral life, which has intrinsic worth. These are duties requiring discipline and commitment – the sort of self-mastery that, as we shall see in Chapter 8, defines good moral character.

In the *Foundations* Kant did hold that we may have an *indirect* duty to tend to our own happiness when the "press of cares" and "unsatisfied wants" tempt us to neglect our duties, but in such cases the end is not our happiness but our morality (399). Moreover, this is only an occasional duty, not a continuing duty like the maxim to cultivate our abilities, a maxim we apparently can never fulfill to the extent that we may say we no longer need to be concerned about it.

In the *Foundations,* all four of Kant's examples of how the Formula of Universal Law tests proposed maxims for embodied moral agents require us to regard some end or other as morally obligatory (421–3). The first two concern our duties to ourselves and the second two our duties to others. The contingent fact that a person may not *care* about one or another morally obligatory natural end is irrelevant to the *use* of such ends to test the morality of that person's maxim. It may, however, be relevant to the person's moral character, if it shows that the motive to adopt and act (or not to do so) on a particular maxim is based not on reason but on desires.

The second example, of borrowing money with no intention of repaying it (422), is only a variation of the maxim of lying promises, and we have already examined the fourth, the maxim of neither contributing to the welfare of others nor asking for their help (423). Kant's other two examples of morally unacceptable maxims also depend on their generating a contradiction with one or another morally obligatory end.

In his first example Kant contended that we have a strict negative duty not to commit suicide only in order to avoid a life promising more pain than pleasure (422).[8] He argued that the maxim of arbitrarily destroying one's own life (and capacity for morally good character) from the motive of self-love, if made a universal law, would generate a teleological contradiction with the role the same self-love already has: "to impel the improvement of life." That is why people contemplating suicide are typically so ambivalent: they find themselves torn between preserving and destroying their own life. Because the maxim under review generates just this kind of contradiction, Kant concluded that it could not function as a law in a possible moral world; it "wholly contradicts the supreme principle of all duty" (422).

The third example in the *Foundations* concerns deliberately neglecting to develop our natural abilities, particularly our mental powers. Under the right conditions, a maxim of doing so *could* also be a universal law (as Kant thought actually was the case with "the South Sea Islanders") without generating a contradiction. Yet he maintained that as rational beings, we "cannot possibly *will*" that such a maxim should be a universal law (423). As we have seen when examining Kant's fourth example a few pages ago, insofar as we are rational as well as finite, we necessarily will to use whatever means are known to be necessary to fulfill our legitimate natural needs. Moreover, to fulfill our moral interests, we also must "regard the development of our talents as a duty" (401n; see 423).[9] But because of his emphasis on negative duties, Kant did not elaborate on the positive side of this duty in the *Foundations*. Like all other positive duties, the obligation to promote our natural perfection allows us latitude to judge exactly how to do so. What is forbidden, Kant held, is the teleological contradiction generated by the maxim that we completely neglect the development of our talents.

KANT'S DOCTRINE CONCERNING LIES

Lying promises are a kind of lie, and Kant's attitude toward lying has often been criticized as excessively rigorous. It is appropriate, then, to digress here to see what he said about lying in other works. Obviously, lies that injure others violate our duty of benevolence. But what about those that do not harm others? When we use the first formula to see if a maxim of telling harmless lies could "harmonize with itself if everyone, in every case, made it a universal law," we generate the following conjunction:

> I will tell lies that do not harm anyone and may have good
> consequences, and I will a world in which everyone tells
> such lies.

Kant held that the notion of lying makes sense only when
the purpose of at least some kinds of speech is understood to
be the communication of information. The logical consequence
of the conjunction above is this contradiction: everyone will
use the same kinds of assertions in order to communicate both
truth and falsehoods. In such a world we could never know
when any such verbal behavior counted as "telling the truth";
and if that were so, then it would also no longer be possible
for anyone to tell a lie. The essential evil of lying therefore lies
in the maxim itself, regardless of motives for and consequences
of telling lies. Deception typically aims at manipulating others
by treating them merely as tools for the liar's purposes, even if
the deception is done from a benevolent motive.

Consider for a moment, Kant in effect wrote, a civil society
with a law permitting, perhaps even mandating, lying for
"good" reasons. Such a law would completely undermine the
credibility of all contracts and promises, thereby undermining
any guarantees of civil rights as well as the very possibility of
a just political system. Because lying "vitiates the source of
[civil] law," Kant held that it must be ranked among the worst
moral evils, wronging "mankind generally."

Since moral prohibitions are unconditional laws, the constraint against lying allows *no* exceptions, no matter how necessary a particular lie may seem. The infamous Machiavelli had
advised the prince to lie "if that is necessary" to stay in power.
Kant was convinced that "necessity has no law" and that once
we accept "necessity" as an excuse for *any* exceptions to the
moral law, eventually it will sanction the violation of every
moral rule.

In this matter, however, it is important to note that the rule
"I may never lie" is not equivalent to the rule "I must always
tell the truth"; we do not have a corresponding positive – and

ridiculous – obligation to tell *everything* we know to *everyone* at *every* opportunity. In his lectures on ethics, Kant had pointed out the value of discretion, that is, prudent reserve in expressing one's thoughts and feelings. We have a moral right to the privacy of our own thoughts, he wrote, a right we should also respect in others. There are usually many morally acceptable ways in which we may avoid telling the truth without telling a lie, including simple silence, noncommittal answers, evasions, and equivocations. As Kant also sensibly recognized, much of our verbal behavior has some point other than the transmission of factual information. Common courtesies and gestures of affection for others are only role-playing; they are not deceptions, "because everyone knows how to take them."

This, then, is what Kant's view about lying comes down to: we may never lie after we have stated outright that we will tell the truth. Honest but discreet people speak the truth but not necessarily the whole truth; by contrast, dishonest persons deliberately say what they know is false because they wish to deceive.

ANOTHER EXAMPLE

Let us now return to the case we saw at the end of Chapter 2, both to show how that judgment should have been made and to clarify the role that natural but morally obligatory ends play in the ordinary moral decisions of human life, particularly to determine our positive and wide moral obligations. Perhaps even more important, the example will show that we have considerable moral latitude in constructing our lives, for the universality and absoluteness of the Categorical Imperative are softened by the fact that its positive mandates are concerned with great generalities and its negative commands only set the boundaries or limits of our moral lives.

So let us reopen the case of a person wanting to become a philosopher because that person finds philosophizing both an important and an agreeable activity. Let us add the further detail that the same person also wants to teach philosophy, say, in Palo Alto, California. Moving to Palo Alto has no obvious relevance to any morally obligatory ends and, unless some can be shown, is not a moral issue at all. But the maxim of becoming a philosopher clearly falls under the obligatory natural end of developing our talents.

Because the Categorical Imperative is fundamentally a negative test, we may begin by asking if the Categorical Imperative forbids anyone to adopt the maxim of developing one's talents by becoming a philosopher if one so wishes. To answer this question, we obviously need to know some things about people and about the world. A maxim preventing everyone from trying to become a philosopher is clearly incompatible with the general obligation and right to develop our talents. There is no inconsistency, however, between our wide obligation to develop our talents, particularly our mental abilities, and a positive permissive law allowing anyone wanting to become a philosopher to try to do so.

We should note that in this test the Categorical Imperative does not *require* that anyone go into philosophy. Nor is it relevant to the test that not many people will want to take up philosophy as a career. (Obviously, it would be *imprudent* for *everyone* to try to take up philosophy as a career.) The test determines, on the basis of the logical requirement of noncontradiction, only that there is no moral objection to those of us wanting to do so to act on our desire. We may therefore conclude it is not morally forbidden and so is morally permissible for a person – any person who wants to do so – to study to become a philosopher.

If the individual's situation is uncomplicated and there are no other relevant moral questions to be raised, this is as far into the decision process as the Categorical Imperative can take us. The moral law does not tell us either *what* we must do to develop our talents or *how* we must do so. As is the case whenever we wish to make morally permissible choices intelligently, we now must turn to prudential considerations.

Once we do so, we have what Kant called a "moral title" to choose as we wish; we have "elbowroom" or "play room" within which to make our decision. We need to figure out what we want most to do, given the various possibilities. Taking circumstances and consequences into account now is not only not immoral but necessary if we are to make as rational a decision as possible. What we decide to do depends on us and on conditions in the world. We need to ask questions like: Do I have sufficient talent and perseverance to be successful? Will jobs in philosophy probably be available after I earn my degree? And so on. Whatever the eventual decision, we can never be certain that we have made the best choice. Such judgments always leave us with some uncertainty.

Nonetheless, we still are well advised to consider the most likely consequences. If a person found out that schools probably would not be hiring instructors for the next several decades, it would be prudent to consider other possibilities. If one determined that there was *no* way to make a living teaching philosophy, it could then be argued that trying to do so would be incompatible with the general obligation of self-preservation, in which case one would have a moral duty to consider a different career. There are many different ways in which one can fulfill the general obligation to develop one's talents. We can, of course, complicate the story, say, by introducing a sudden inheritance, but there is no reason to think that Kant's procedures cannot accommodate such ingenious casuistry.

If we reflect on how people make such decisions when they try to do so conscientiously and thoughtfully, we can understand why Kant thought he was doing just what he said he intended to do: explicate our ordinary practical reasoning. Further, Kant is correct, in this case at least, in maintaining that the Categorical Imperative is not all that difficult to use.

61

NOTES

1. The laws of the moral world of freedom cannot, of course, hold in the same manner as physical laws do in the causally determined world of experience. Were they to do so, they would transform the world of freedom into a deterministic world, thereby destroying morality.
2. When using the Categorical Imperative, we should not use the verbs "want" and "wish" in place of "will," for the first two verbs belong to the vocabulary of desires.
3. Kant slipped up in 403 when he added that those who overhastily believe such promises "would pay me back in my own coin." As he himself repeatedly insisted, consideration of adverse consequences is a prudential, not a moral, matter.
4. This analysis also does not address the question, Can situations arise in which I may break a promise I originally made in good faith? Thus it does not result in a "duty of promise keeping." Here the Categorical Imperative tells us only that we may not make lying promises.

    Nor does the moral rejection of lying promises of itself also imply that there must be a *practice* of promise making and keeping. However, elsewhere Kant held that we are not morally free to give up a world with either promises or truthful statements. Even when no particular individual is injured, Kant wrote, lies and lying promises set us "in opposition to the condition and means through which any human society is possible."
5. Three remarks need to be made about this case. First, it is important not to misrepresent Kant as offering a prudential argument that we should help others *in order* to get their help in return. Second, the argument here would not hold in a moral world of rational agents who do not share our needs and dependencies. That is why there is reason to qualify general claims here by expressions like a "moral world of human beings." In this case what is "rational" is not a *purely* rational matter but certainly *is* what is rational for vulnerable beings like ourselves. Finally, the same type of argument can be used to show the immorality of the state of nature, in which violence is unrestrained and individual life has little value; such a condition systematically undermines our ability to flourish as free autonomous agents.
6. In the first section of the *Foundations* Kant described the good will as the *only* thing "good without qualification," so there may be

some surprise because he later introduced obligatory ends such as personhood.

The idea of "persons" includes whatever other rational beings there might be, but since the only such beings of which we have knowledge are human persons, we have duties only to them. However, Kant also held that we do have duties *with regard to* other beings that are still duties to ourselves. For example, we should not wantonly destroy beauty in nature and we should not unnecessarily inflict pain on animals, not because destruction and pain are moral evils (they are natural evils), but because such conduct tends to weaken our moral disposition. Elsewhere he also maintained that we do not have special duties to God, for we cannot *know* that God exists or, if he does, whether he has revealed his will.

7. Elsewhere, Kant held that our positive obligation to preserve our physical integrity entails a correlative, negative duty not to do anything that might contribute to or cause the destruction of our physical well-being, such as the excessive consumption of food or drink. But, this does not mean that he believed it is *always* immoral to risk our lives, for we may have to do so in order to act according to duty. Nor did he portray the positive duty of self-preservation as narrow, requiring us to do everything possible to stay alive.

8. Some critics have thought Kant's argument here to be weak. As he presents this case, the conflict is within self-love. If, as Kant thought, the purpose of self-love is always to gain pleasure and avoid pain, there seems no obvious contradiction in saying, "I will promote my existence as long as it provides more pleasure than pain." What about a case in which a person considers suicide out of a sense of self-respect? If, for example, one can foresee that, under torture or due to dementing illness (such as Alzheimer's disease), one eventually will lose all rationality and behave in ways seriously incompatible with self-respect, the historical continuity of the self would seem to entail *some* present responsibility for preventing such a state.

In his *Metaphysics of Morals*, however, Kant produced another argument against suicide, based on our duty to sustain our capacity for moral action. He argued that a maxim of committing suicide out of duty is self-contradictory, for it affirms both that we are subject to duty and that we also should withdraw from all duty, both that we have incomparable worth and that we can deliberately destroy that worth. "Man cannot renounce his personality as long as he is a subject of duty, hence so long as he lives," he wrote.

He also offered a case in which he seemed to imply that suicide would be impermissible even to avoid the madness then inevitably caused by rabies.

9. Self-development for beings like us, Kant held, requires qualitative development, not quantitative perfection; that is, we do not need to try to know *everything* to fulfill this obligation.

Kant may have experienced some tension here between his Pietistic background and his deep commitment to the Enlightenment. We see one side of Kant in 403–4, where he insists that "ordinary moral reasoning" needs little formal education in order to be a competent and even subtle moral guide. But, taken alone, that discussion is misleading, for Kant also believed that moral development presupposes some cultural development. Education *of itself* will not automatically make us morally better people; it may only give us greater potential for reprehensible behavior. Good moral character still depends on the development of the will. However, it is also true that the more educated we are, usually the greater is our *capacity* for autonomy and for contributing to such morally good ends as helping others.

4

THE FORMULA OF RESPECT FOR
THE DIGNITY OF PERSONS

THE first formula is a completely formal test, requiring that
maxims can be willed as universal laws, that is, as laws for
all rational beings. By contrast, the second is not purely formal,
for it introduces the notion of "humanity": we are required to
respect the freedom and ability of each person to make his or
her own decision.[1] Probably the best-known version of the second formula is this: "Act so that you treat humanity, whether
in your own person or in the person of any other, always as
an end and never as a means only" (429; see 433).

In Chapter 1, we discussed Kant's protest against tyranny, in
which the ruler uses his subjects merely as instruments to carry
out his will. By contrast, Kant offered a political theory of the
people, based on the moral Universal Principle of Justice: everyone has a fundamental dignity simply as a person, and no
one has the moral right to interfere with the lawful freedom
of others or to use them *merely* for his or her own purposes.
This is just what the second formula enjoins.

Kant's stress in the second formula on the intrinsic equal
value of each person does, in fact, enunciate a fundamental
moral, political, and religious principle presupposed in the ordinary moral judgments of nearly everyone today. It has a maj-
esty that can so fire the moral sensibilities of his readers as to
make the second formula seem both obviously right and the
most appealing version of the Categorical Imperative.

Given the political power of both the civil and religious au-
thorities at the time he was writing, it must have taken some
courage for Kant to propose what many of his readers would

have regarded as a radical and dangerous doctrine. On one occasion he, in fact, did find it necessary to defend his doctrine against the objection that it promotes an attitude smacking of arrogance and self-conceit and violates the ordinary person's obligation to be humble in the presence of authority.

RELATION TO THE FIRST FORMULA

Kant held that, despite the addition of the notion of "humanity" in the second formula, the two formulas are "at bottom the same," the second being but a different way to "represent" the first (see 436–7). The very fact that the first formula is a principle of reciprocity, requiring that maxims be capable of being universal law, means that it does implicitly recognize that rational beings all have objective, intrinsic worth (434). The second formula restates the requirement of justice by insisting that we may not act in ways that deny respect to anyone, ourselves included, and thus it generates the same moral judgments about the requirements of justice as the first.

The second formula, however, explicitly recognizes that, as persons, we humans are not only rational beings but also physical beings with emotions, which add a special dimension to human morality. Although Kant hoped this formula would bring "an Idea of reason closer to intuition" (436), the very formality of the first formula led him to hold that it is more fundamental than the second (431), and he himself preferred it to the second (436–7).

Like the first, the second formula is a norm of impartiality that abstracts from all the information that underlies our subjective preferences. The notion of a human person in this formula, therefore, is as impersonal as the idea of universal law. In Chapter 1 we saw how the disinterested and impersonal character of the notion of personhood provides the moral basis for a society in which the administration of justice is not skewed by personal relationships and the law can be administered in an impartial manner. The impersonality of the notion of persons has led to this part of Kant's doctrine being described as "an ethics for relations between strangers." It also accounts for Kant's regarding the second formula initially as a negative norm, like the Principle of Justice in his political philosophy. The concept of persons "must be conceived only negatively" (437); persons are "an end against which we should never act" (437; see 430). They limit the ways in which we may satisfy our desires.

But ethics goes beyond politics, and it would be ethically inadequate to fulfill *only* the negative command, for we can do that merely by avoiding others and being indifferent to them. So, like the first formula, the second also tells us we have positive duties both to ourselves and to others (423, 430). Both the negative and the positive injunctions are stressed in that version of the second formula, which commands every person to "treat himself and all others, never merely as a means, but in every case at the same time as an end in himself" (433). Kant elsewhere called this formula both "the ethical law of perfection," since our main positive duty to ourselves is to enhance our own moral integrity, and "the principle of benevolence," since our positive duties to others concern mainly contributing to their welfare.

PERSONS AND THINGS

When he explained this formula, Kant wrote movingly of the radical difference between persons and mere things.

If things have any value at all, Kant wrote, their value is only extrinsic, conditional, and subjective. That is, things – whether they are products of nature or artifacts – have value only insofar as someone or other happens to regard them as valuable, either for their utility (their "market price") or for emotional reasons (their "affection price"; see 434–5). Things, therefore, all have a price, determined by what people will give and take in exchange for them, and in that context money is regarded as the ultimate standard of value.[2] Because they are only relatively valuable, that is, valuable only to those wanting them, things can provide the basis only for hypothetical imperatives (428). If categorical imperatives are to be possible, then, there must be something of intrinsic and absolute value, worthwhile just for what it is (as an "end in itself").[3]

At this point in his argument Kant wrote, "Now I say that . . . ," meaning, "What I now wish to claim is that . . . " (428). Since he was leaving the defense of his analysis to the last section of the *Foundations,* in effect he proceeded to offer only the following hypothetical claim. If there are any such beings with intrinsic worth, they can have that worth only if they are good, not in the sense that they might be desirable to someone or other, but good according to standards that hold for every being with reason. Further, we humans are such beings, and that is why we are called "persons." We have objective worth; we *ought* to be regarded as an "end" for everyone (435; see 428–9, 434–6).

To say that persons are objective ends is to say that, unlike things, they absolutely *should* be regarded as having worth, whether or not they also are desired as contributing to anyone's happiness (428). Persons are "self-existent" ends, having worth simply because they exist (428, 437). What gives us this worth, Kant wrote, is our "humanity," that is, our moral personality, making us far superior to mere animals. They are led by their instincts, but we are free and autonomous; we are self-legislating subjects in whom the moral law resides (435–6).

Because he was not trying to offer a scientific description, this claim does not, and as we shall see in Chapter 10, cannot, rest on any empirical information. In that sense it admits of no proof (430–1).

The intrinsic worth of all persons is an ethical idea that Kant inherited from Christianity. But since he was trying to construct a moral view based on reason, not on faith, he could not adopt it without some revision. He therefore struggled to find new language in which to convey his claim. Stylistically, the expression he adopted – each person is "an end in himself" – is particularly ugly (428). It can be confusing as well, for Kant also used the term "end" to refer to what we might want to produce or control; that is obviously not what he meant by the word here (427, 437).

We can be and often are regarded as having conditional value, insofar as we are considered to be useful, likable, lovable, or admirable. Because we are dependent beings, we do have both the need and the right, subject to moral limitations, to attend to our own needs and the needs of those we care about, and to do so we often must use each other. Likewise, when we think of people in terms of their skills and abilities, as in business, we regard them as more or less "marketable" and their time as having a price (434–5). Kant did *not* think that this is morally wrong and he in fact defined "worldly wisdom" as "the skill to influence others in order to use them for one's own ends" (416n).

However, regarding ourselves or others *only* as having extrinsic value *is* wrong, for our worth is not dependent just on our usefulness or desirability (428). Because we are subject to the moral law, the ultimate source of all worth, each and every one of us has an absolute and irreplaceable dignity, beyond all price (435–6). That is why the expression "Everyone has her price" denigrates a person so viciously. What the second formula stipulates is that we may not regard or treat others or allow ourselves to be treated *only* as instrumentally valuable, *merely* as a means to satisfy someone's desires, *merely* as a source of pleasure. We may never renounce our right to respect, and we ought never to act so as to reduce ourselves or others to the status of mere things. Persons demand respect just by being persons, and that means not acting on a rule that treats any person merely as a thing. Consequently, as the first formula requires, we need to ask, Could my maxim also be a law, holding not just for myself but for everyone else as well?

Since we are only contingently moral, we may not *want* to recognize that everyone else is our moral equal, and Kant therefore described respect for persons as "necessary" in the sense of being morally obligatory. We have an unconditional duty to recognize the dignity of every person, contrary, if necessary, to any feelings we may have of indifference or aversion. All contingent facts about others as well as any relationships we may have with them are irrelevant both to their inherent value and to the respect we owe them. Unlike the emotions of affection and dislike, the moral law neither shows preference for nor excludes any particular persons or groups.

We may have special grounds for respecting individuals who exemplify the moral law in their lives (435), and we may also lose respect for individuals whose actions lead us to infer that they have a morally bad character. But the fundamental respect owed persons is not based on merit or achievement, not even on morally good character. Kant insisted that even a moral reprobate is still inescapably subject to the moral law and so still is owed respect for being autonomous, that is, for having the *capacity* to develop a morally good will (454–5).[4]

RESPECT FOR PERSONS

Before examining the specific duties that he derived from the second formula, we need to mention several other points in Kant's analysis of the notion of respect for persons.

Given the historical context within which he was writing, Kant was particularly concerned lest we confuse the notion of respect with that of the honor traditionally given the aristocracy and the powerful. Honor rests on societal roles and distinctions, whereas respect is an attitude (and conduct displaying that attitude) due a person, regardless of social position, occupation, learning, wealth, accomplishments, or any other special qualities or talents he or she may or may not possess. For the same reason, respect should not be confused with pride in one's own qualities or a similar appreciation of the uniqueness of others. Respect rests on the fact that the moral law resides in the reason of each and every person alike, who therefore is capable of moral self-determination and has the ability to attain the highest achievable good, a good will. The respect owed persons, then, is owed to them only because persons are the bearers of the moral law (401n, 435–6).

Whereas morality must be based only on reason alone, not on feelings, self-respect and respect for all others *are* moral feelings, and feelings so critical to human moral life that Kant identified them as the subjective foundation of all human morality. We do not have a duty just to *have* respect for persons, he held, since that feeling arises irresistibly within us after we have recognized their moral nature (399). What the second formula does require of us is that we work at deepening our sensitivity to the importance of self-respect and respect for others.

Besides stressing the objective and intrinsic worth of persons, therefore, the second formula has another, equally important function. It emphasizes why *we* must be moral: in order to live up to the dignity we have by virtue of being a person, to sustain the right we have to moral self-esteem. Whenever we act immorally, we treat ourselves merely as instrumentalities, merely as a thing.

DUTIES TO SELF

In his discussion of the second formula, Kant reexamined the examples he had already used, this time from the point of view of self-respect and respect for others. The first and third examples concern duties to self.

In the first, adopting the maxim of committing suicide to escape from a painful condition would mean regarding ourselves merely as a means to an extrinsic good, a prudentially tolerable quality of life, and we then radically undervalue our intrinsic worth (429, 449–50).[5] Such a maxim produces a contradiction: it promotes happiness, which ultimately gets its value only from its relation to us, and also advocates the destruction of the source of that value, namely, ourselves, thereby banishing morality itself from the world insofar as it is in our power to do so.

In the third example Kant allowed that not adopting a maxim of developing our physical and mental abilities does not necessarily imply using ourselves merely as a means and so may not directly conflict with our self-respect.[6] But even if such a decision does not violate our negative obligations concerning "the preservation of humanity as an end in itself," it still is not compatible with the respect we should have for ourselves as free, rational beings (430; see 423). Consequently, a policy of such neglect is morally unacceptable. How we fulfill the coordinate positive duty to perfect our humanity depends on contingencies that cannot be taken into account ahead of time. Kant strongly supported the development of effective educational techniques but in the *Foundations* suggested only that students be taught to think about "the worth of the things which they might possibly adopt as ends" (415). We will return to this duty in Chapter 9.

We have other relevant negative duties to ourselves. Miserly avarice, for example, violates self-respect because it means regarding our existence as valuable only as a means to the accumulation of mere things, and it often also means refusing to spend what we have to get what we need to fulfill our duties. Servility characterizes any attitude or action by which we treat ourselves merely as a means to curry another's favor; it thereby disavows the respect we should have for ourselves. Likewise, the immoderate consumption of food and drink and the use of drugs for nonmedicinal purposes violate self-respect insofar as they impair our ability to act rationally and morally.

OUR MORAL VOCATION

Kant began the first section of the *Foundations* with the claim that nothing "can be taken as good without qualification" except a morally virtuous character, or what he called "a good will" (393).[7] Clearly then, if we respect ourselves as we should, our main positive obligation to ourselves is to strive constantly for a morally good character.

This means, of course, doing what is required by the Categorical Imperative. In his political philosophy Kant called behavior, considered apart from its motivation, that conforms to the Principle of Law "lawful" or "legal": the maxim of an action is lawful if it is a maxim anyone could adopt, or, in Kant's words, if "it can coexist with everyone's freedom in accordance with a universal law." Such actions are also *morally* legal – "moral in form," "morally good in letter," and "according to duty."

Simply performing lawful actions may support a just public order, but it is not sufficient for the *person* performing such actions thereby to merit the judgment of being, to that extent at least, a morally good individual (397–8). If an action does not conflict with the Categorical Imperative but is done from an "ulterior" or nonmoral incentive, to satisfy some desire or aversion, then the action itself may not be morally wrong, but, in abstraction from other considerations, it also has no moral worth. It is only a contingent accident that the action is legally correct; it just happens to be the morally correct thing to do. An action is morally good in spirit or intention only if one chooses that action *because* it is what one ought morally to do. We therefore have the obligation to do our duty from the motive of duty.

As we have also seen, Kant further claimed that moral worth depends on the intention, not the accomplishment. A good will is good "only because of its willing" (394; see 399–401, 435, 437, 439). The reason is that our efforts to achieve our aims are so often frustrated, both by our own limited abilities and by conditions in the world. If our ability to act dutifully were similarly limited, moral imperatives could hold only conditionally. That would make the notion of a *categorical* imperative meaningless and would destroy the notion of morality itself.[8] But, as we have already seen, we can always shape our *intentions* in a morally acceptable manner, and our inability to carry out those intentions does not necessarily detract from our moral quality (439).

We obviously do not satisfy the demands of morality by insincere wishes; we must always strive with all our power to carry out our moral decisions in our conduct (394). External performances can have moral significance as a sign of the sincerity of our moral disposition. But what essentially makes a person morally good, Kant argued, is that person's intentions, those "inner actions" that precede and cause our physical movements as their effects (if the latter are not frustrated by conditions over which we have no control).[9] To act in an ethically worthy fashion, we must have what Kant described as a "submissive disposition" and a "moral attitude" that motivates us to act "from duty," "out of respect for" and "for the sake of" the moral law (390, 398–401, 435).

The morally best character we can attain, Kant thought, is what he called the good or dutiful or conscientious will. The term he used most frequently was one he borrowed from the Stoics, one also not much used today: "virtue," meaning both power and self-mastery. The good person must have the moral strength and courage to constrain himself or herself to act dutifully.[10] Like the idea of duty, the notion of virtue implies a continual propensity to act immorally, so good moral character requires a continuing commitment to the moral law within us. Virtuous character, therefore, depends on the exercise of freedom in both its negative and its positive meanings: negatively, the power systematically to judge and act independently of and, if necessary, contrary to all the desires and inclinations we may have; and positively, the self-mastery to bring our decisions under the moral law and to motivate us to act from a dutiful attitude (444).[11]

Because it is our own reason that categorically commands us to do our duty from the motive of duty, we must believe that we always can do so. However, we simply can never be certain, even in a single instance, that we actually *have* acted from the motive of duty (406–7); what we can be more positive about is that we have *tried* to act dutifully. For this reason, as strange as this may sound, Kant held that, strictly speaking, we are not bound to *act* from the motive of duty but we are bound to adopt the *maxim* of acting from the motive of duty and then strive with all the power we have actually to do so.

Kant had a sensitive appreciation of the moral frailty of human nature. Even when we are committed to acting conscientiously, he wrote, we still are only contingently morally good. We are never so confirmed in virtue that we can be confident we will not fail morally in the future, and we always need to be apprehensive about doing so. Since even the best of us will have moral lapses, we need to reaffirm our moral resolve frequently.

PURSUING HAPPINESS

Since Kant so often treated the Categorical Imperative as a negative criterion, determining what we must not do in the pursuit of happiness, it is easy to overlook Kant's insistence that happiness is our highest natural good – actually an essential part of our total final good – and that we have a right to tend to our morally permissible happiness and welfare. We therefore should not try to renounce our concern for our own well-being; in fact, we are incapable of doing so.

However, given Kant's analysis of the notion of "duty" as implying reluctance on our part, he did hold that we do not have a direct duty to promote our happiness, arguing that it does not make sense to say that we have an obligation to do what we will do inevitably and spontaneously. But to fulfill our positive duty to strive for good moral character, we may find ourselves *indirectly* obligated to tend to our happiness (399). This can be the case, for example, if doing so means we can more easily attend to our moral obligations, if adversity, pain, and want are great temptations to transgress our duty, or if the concept of happiness becomes so indefinite that we begin to neglect proper diet and exercise.[12] But in all such cases, the end is not happiness but the agent's morality.

RESPECT FOR OTHERS

Just as we have a right to the respect of others, so too they have an equal right to our respect. What the Formula of Respect for the Dignity of Persons requires of us is to recognize that all other persons are, negatively, "the supreme limiting condition of all subjective ends" (431). These negative duties are emphasized in that version of the formula that states: "A rational being, as by its nature an end and thus an end in itself, must serve in every maxim as the condition restricting all merely relative and arbitrary ends" (436). We must limit what we do in the pursuit of happiness by refraining from acting in ways that would endanger or violate anyone else's autonomy and self-respect (437).[13] Whenever we do use others to promote our own welfare, we may not humiliate them or fail to recognize that they have a dignity equal to our own.

In his second example in the *Foundations,* that of making false promises considered from the viewpoint of the second formula, Kant pointed out that, like physical violence and theft, such promises use another person *only* as a thing, only as a means to one's own end, by refusing to recognize that the other person is also an autonomous agent. Lying promises treat the other person in a way in which that person could not assent as a person with self-respect: such a person could not rationally consent to the purpose of the lying promise – to be deceived or manipulated (429–30). Once again, this means acting only on maxims that can be willed as laws in a moral world.

Some commentators have concluded, therefore, that Kant was simply offering a variation of the Golden Rule. But in 430n he explicitly argued against interpreting the Categorical Imperative in this way. Even when stated as a negative norm (and so in its strictest form), the Golden Rule has crucial flaws. It is concerned only with how we treat others and ignores duties to self; moreover, in the case of positive duties to others it does not insist on either the respect owed others or duties of benevolence to them, and in the case of negative duties to others, it is vague enough to be understood to be merely a norm of prudential reciprocity.[14]

Positively, respect for others means recognizing and appreciating their interests (430). Every human being, Kant held, has two necessary ends or interests. As moral beings, we are obligated to strive for our own moral well-being, that is, virtue; and as moral beings with a physical nature, we all inevitably want natural well-being, that is, happiness.

Because no one can do for another what only that person can do, Kant held that we are not obligated to assume the responsibility for another's moral character.[15] Nevertheless, we do have a positive obligation to recognize and promote, insofar as we can, their pursuit of happiness. We have just seen that we usually do not have a duty to care about and try to promote our own happiness, because we will inevitably do so. But we do not necessarily care about the happiness of others, and we can easily be tempted to ignore the legitimate interests of others while pursuing our own happiness. Since the Categorical Imperative allows us to adopt only maxims that are fit to serve as universal laws, we are morally entitled to pursue our own otherwise morally permissible happiness only if we also empathically identify with and contribute, insofar as we can, to others' pursuit of their morally permissible happiness.

Kant summarized this obligation as a "law of love" but then quickly added that we need to understand the term "love" rightly. According to his view, we do not have a duty to feel sympathy for others, for we cannot feel emotions like solicitude merely on command, nor should our duties to others be based on feelings. Rather, *moral* love is not an emotion but a practical attitude about how we should *act* toward others, regardless of whether or not we *feel* any affection for them (399).[16] Our moral obligation to contribute to the happiness of others rests fundamentally on respect for them as persons, rather than on their happiness being of special personal concern to us (441).

More specifically, what moral love requires of us is that we adopt a maxim of benevolence or well-wishing that does not allow us to be completely indifferent to others but instead requires us to be concerned about others' desires and needs. Again, according to the moral requirement of universal law, it is morally permissible for us to be benevolent toward ourselves only if we also are benevolent to all others as well. Therefore, misanthropy is contrary to our obligation of benevolence.

Admittedly, Kant wrote, benevolence alone is not much; it does not actually help anyone. The biblical admonition "Love your neighbor as yourself" means, as Jesus immediately explained, that we should do good to them (399; Matt. 5.44). Benevolence must be practical, that is, show itself in our adopting a maxim of beneficence – of *acting* benevolently, of promoting and contributing to the well-being of others. The ground for the obligation of beneficence, like that of benevolence, lies in the requirement of the first formula that we are morally entitled to be beneficent to ourselves only if we are also beneficent to others, as well as in the requirement of the second formula that morally acceptable maxims must be able to serve as laws in a moral world in which persons are given the respect they deserve.[17]

When Kant considered the fourth example in the *Foundations* from the point of view of the second formula, he argued that we do not show sufficient respect for others if we do not make their interests our own and help them as much as we can. We therefore are morally obligated to contribute to others' ability to live as rational but vulnerable agents, even if that means sacrificing at least part of our own well-being (430).

BENEVOLENCE AND BENEFICENCE

The negative requirement to refrain from violating the respect due others is a universal law; we may not treat *anyone* with disrespect. The *positive* obligation of respect for others is also a universal requirement, but, like all positive, wide duties, it requires us only to adopt and act on the *maxim* of concern for the well-being of others. Because it mandates respect for persons just as persons, the moral law does not and cannot discriminate between persons. For that reason, Kant held that a moral theory simply cannot specify ahead of time the exact ways in which we should fulfill each of our positive obligations. All the universal moral law can do is prescribe that we may not completely ignore the maxim of concern for others.

Universal benevolence or well-wishing requires very little, only that we wish everyone well. As for beneficence or well-doing, Kant held that we do not violate the universality of the maxim of concern for others if we choose to help some persons and projects rather than others. For one thing, we clearly are not obliged to sacrifice our happiness completely by trying to contribute to the happiness of others. The universal maxim of doing that generates a practical absurdity. For another, since each of us has limited resources and power, we are not obligated to contribute to the well-being of every human being, nor are we obligated to a kind of moral egalitarianism in which we would have to contribute equally to the well-being of everyone. Only God has the resources to be beneficent to everyone.

Kant did not try to tell us what features about others we *must* regard as relevant to a decision about how to act. Such matters must be left up to each person's judgment, to be decided on the basis of considerations such as our ongoing concerns and commitments as well as the extent of our resources and the severity of the needs of others. In books other than the *Foundations* he also suggested that differences in social rank, age, sex, health, economic situation, education, and even personality all might be taken into account legitimately.

He also showed his sensitivity to our ordinary moral convictions by proposing that, in general, we should try to help those closest to us. Other factors being equal, there is nothing morally wrong in giving more weight to the concerns of people to whom we have emotional or familial ties. According to his view, for example, it certainly would be morally permissible for a person to choose to save the life of a family member rather than that of a stranger.

Finally, since we are closest to ourselves (in every sense), we are *not* bound literally to love others as we love ourselves; "even according to duty" we are morally permitted to tend to our own needs first. So duties to ourselves have more prima facie weight than our duties to others.

NOTES

1. Kant held that since the only persons we know are humans, they are the only persons to whom we have moral obligations. Many critical moral problems in medicine raise the question whether it is legitimate for us to regard some living beings as human but not as persons. Among the problematic cases are fetuses, the profoundly retarded, and the irrevocably senile or comatose. Kant is of little help here, for he held there are no facts that can function as identifying criteria for the purely rational and empirically empty idea of a person.
2. Kant did not consider cases in which some things – like art masterpieces, endangered species, and a fragile environment – are irreplaceable and for that reason are regarded as beyond all price.
3. When Kant wrote that persons are "the ground of a possible cat-

egorical imperative" (428), he was not claiming that the Categorical Imperative itself is based on the objective value of persons. What he meant was that if there were no persons, there would be no moral law.

4. The expression "a good will" in 455 must mean the individual is still autonomous and under the moral law even if he does not actually have a good character.

5. Kant's condemnation of suicide should not be interpreted as identifying personhood with life; of itself life is simply a natural, not an absolute, good. In most cases, the promotion of virtue clearly does require the protection of life and health; but in other cases we could have a duty to risk the loss of our life. (Kant tacitly allowed killing in some wars, and he explicitly advocated capital punishment.)

6. Perhaps Kant was thinking of the uneducated peasants he knew; the Prussian state severely limited what they could hope to make of themselves but they still possessed moral reason and the possibility of moral virtue.

7. Actually, a morally good character is not good in every possible respect. When morality requires us to sacrifice our natural welfare, virtue cannot be considered prudentially good. But this is a judgment that morality requires us to ignore; virtue or a good will must still be considered the supreme and incomparable human good.

8. Kant is often quoted as maintaining that "should implies can." Although he nowhere made this claim in so many words, it was clearly his doctrine, since we can always form our intentions according to the requirements of the Categorical Imperative. The aphorism is often misinterpreted to mean that moral obligations are conditioned by physical possibilities, so that being unable to repay a debt would release us from our moral obligation to do so. What Kant did mean to claim is that the sheer fact of physical ability or inability does not alter the moral dispositions we should have.

9. Kant used many different terms to refer to a person's intention, including "volition," "willing," "the maxim of the will," "the determination of the will," "the inner legislation of reason," "the principle of volition," "the mental disposition," and "character" (see 394, 412, 416).

10. Their different analyses of the role of emotions in human moral life led to a corresponding difference in the moral ideals Aristotle and Kant presented. Kant thought that Aristotle's ideal of moral excellence and his analysis of practical wisdom were merely fantasy: We cannot habituate our emotions to love what is right

(rather than what is merely pleasurable), as Aristotle had claimed, and if we could, we should not do so, since behavior based on emotions is heteronomous. Aristotle, however, judged that the virtuous or morally strong person – Kant's morally best person – is only the second-best, not the best, person we can become.

Throughout the *Foundations* Kant portrayed virtue as our highest possible moral accomplishment. Later he held that we actually have a vocation to the higher status of holiness, where the will never conflicts with the moral law. Holiness, however, is not something we can attain by our own efforts alone; we need divine assistance, which, incidentally, Kant thought available to us.

11. When Kant described the practical role of pure reason as having an "influence on the will," in effect he was saying that our practical reason or will must be able to be completely self-determining, a law unto itself (396; see 412, 447).

12. The last situation describes the case Kant presents of the man suffering from gout (399), in which (as may often be the case in our own lives) the choice of a single immediate pleasure conflicts with happiness in the sense of the satisfaction of all our inclinations as a whole. If he goes on a diet *not* because he wants to but because he recognizes that he needs to do so for the sake of his health and happiness, his choice now may be based on his indirect duty "to secure one's own happiness"; only then do we have grounds for believing that now "his conduct could have true moral worth."

13. Opposed to our strict obligation to respect others are both attitudes and actions that arise out of envy, ingratitude, malice, pride, or vengefulness, or that treat others as worthless, such as calumny, slander, ridicule, contempt, as well as an arrogance that demands from others a respect it denies them. These violate the respect owed others and also may make it more difficult for them to maintain their own rightful self-respect.

14. Kant's footnote in 430 helps clarify how "treating another only as a means" is equivalent to pursuing an end another person "does not share" and to which that person "cannot possibly agree." Since people can want, adopt, pursue, and share immoral ends, the ends to which Kant referred are only those that others may adopt as autonomous agents.

15. Kant also held that we should avoid scandalous conduct that might adversely affect another's character. Although he did not discuss the possibility that we might have a duty to support others'

pursuit of virtue, he obviously regarded this as a duty he himself had, for he wrote the *Foundations* to help others make their moral judgments correctly (389–90, 405).

16. Note the historical antecedent of moral love in Christian *agapeism*. Moral love, Kant wrote elsewhere, must not be confused either with sexual passion, which has nothing in common with moral love, or with simple affection, which is merely a feeling and is therefore not morally valuable. We do not have a duty to have or not have such feelings, for we cannot generate or get rid of them just by willing to do so or just because we may think we have a duty to do so.

17. Whatever help we give others should be given so as to allow them to keep their self-respect. Helping others should not undermine their ability or deny their obligation to be responsible and self-determining.

5

THE FORMULA OF LEGISLATION
FOR A MORAL COMMUNITY

THE first formula commands us to act autonomously, on maxims fit to serve as the formal structure of a moral world. The second formula commands us to to recognize that all persons have objective value and so are obligatory "matter." Kant called the third formula the most comprehensive variation of the Categorical Imperative, combining both the matter and the form of our moral life (431, 436): "Every rational being must act as if by his maxims he were at all times a legislative member of the universal kingdom of ends" (438; see 431, 434).

THE ROLE OF THE THIRD FORMULA

The third formula presents us with a moral vision of our final and comprehensive collective destiny, thereby satisfying our rational need for an ultimate goal. It is our nature as reasoning beings, Kant wrote, to seek ultimate answers. Partial or tentative answers will not do, for we seek explanations that are comprehensive as well as final. He summarized our quest for finalities by asking three questions. The first was, What can I know? and his answer (in his *Critique of Pure Reason*) was that what we can know is limited to what we can learn through experience, through our senses. The second question was, What ought I to do? and the answer, as we have seen, was, "Fulfill your moral vocation, by adopting and acting on the Law of Autonomy."

The third question was, If I do what I ought to do, what may I then hope? Kant addressed this question most fully in his

Religion within the Limits of Reason Alone. But in the *Foundations,*
the third formula does challenge us to ask what sort of moral
world we should aim to create and also commands us to strive
to realize it. That world should be a community of persons all
acting autonomously, all holding one another in mutual respect (433). Like the kingdom of nature, a kingdom of ends is
also shaped by laws, but, as we saw in Chapter 1, its laws form
the basis for a community of free and equal members (433,
436n, 438).

Although he did not distinguish clearly between them in the
Foundations, Kant held that this moral union is an ideal that
should exist in three distinct forms. First, we can envisage a
civil society in which everyone observes the Principle of Justice,
and that, of course, is the ideal political state. We further can
conceive of a community in which everyone observes the
moral law out of dutifulness; and that ideal, for Kant, is captured in the notion of a religious community framed within the
limits of reason alone. Finally, since our own reason holds that
justice demands that people have the happiness their virtue
merits, we can at least think of an ideal moral world sometime
in the future in which the laws of nature would conform to
the moral law so that people would in fact receive the happiness they deserve.

The Categorical Imperative is, of course, the ultimate norm
that defines the formal relations between the members of all
three unions. It obligates everyone to obey those fundamental
maxims they can rationally prescribe as laws (see 433–4, 438).
As the first formula stresses, those maxims must be universal
laws holding unconditionally; and that means they cannot rest
on any individual's or group's special interests (432). As the
second formula emphasizes, the dignity of each person rests on
the capacity to formulate and adopt such laws, whereas each
person's virtue depends on obedience to those same laws. Thus,
each person is both ruler and subject in each form of the ideal
moral world, since each is both legislator of the Law of Auton-

omy and under that same law (431, 433). (Only God could be sovereign lawgiver yet not also subject to constraint by such legislation; see 434.)

The somewhat ugly title Kant himself settled on, the "kingdom of ends," points to the three different forms this moral ideal should take (433). His calling it a "kingdom" (a *Reich,* often translated today as "realm") hints that it should exist politically, as a state. The title also has religious overtones, recalling the Kingdom of God proclaimed in the Gospels. Those religious connotations point to the second form, an ethical society, as a more adequate embodiment of the moral ideal, as well as to the third form of that union in a future life.

This duty, Kant wrote, cannot be satisfied just by the efforts of individuals concerned only with their own moral lives, for the goal is a collective, social good, not merely an aggregate of the moral achievements of individuals. Therefore, our obligation to promote the kingdom of ends is a special duty, unlike any other. It involves the human species as a whole, requiring each of us to recognize that our moral destiny is inextricably tied to our relations with one another in a communal endeavor.

Because Kant thought the third formula would vivify the meaning of the Categorical Imperative, he hoped it would promote our acceptance of the moral law (436). However, he still recommended that, when making our moral judgments, we should "proceed always in accordance with the strict method" by using the first formula both as our ultimate moral norm and as the ultimate ground for moral motivation (436). He even held that we should *not* use the third formula as our ultimate moral norm, which may be the reason he offered only a few variations of it.[1] For one thing, he worried that doing so could tempt us to take our moral goals to be more fundamental than the moral law itself, and doing that would turn autonomy into heteronomy (see 435–9, 444, 462). (Instead, both the value of persons and the identification of the nature of our moral goals are based on the first formula.) Moreover, the actual achievement of the goals morality sets before us is not completely in our control, whereas our moral worth depends only on what always lies entirely in our own power, namely, intentions formed in obedience to the Law of Autonomy.

THE MORAL COMMUNITY: THE STATE

As we saw in the first chapter, Kant did not believe that the state is either a necessary evil or an impediment to morally permissible freedom. To the contrary, he was convinced that our moral life cannot flourish outside civil society. We saw that the state itself should have a moral foundation, in the Principle of Justice. The third formula obligates us to strive with all our power to promote a republican state in which the dignity of each person is acknowledged and protected (438). Living under absolute monarchs, Kant would not have underestimated the difficulties in bringing about such a state. Thus, he concluded that the moral law imposes on us only a duty to *try* to create and to sustain such a world.

As we also saw in the first chapter, each person within the state still has his or her "private ends," but the state must "abstract from [these] personal differences" to legislate laws that, by holding universally, recognize the ability and responsibility of each person to live a rational, free, and moral life. Juridical obligations therefore should enforce the negative requirement that at least our behavior be legally correct, that is, follow the letter of the moral law by not violating the outer freedom of others. Finally, because the citizens still remain in an "ethical state of nature," indifferent to or hostile to others, laws concerning external duties and rights must all be coercively enforced by the state.

THE ETHICAL COMMUNITY: THE CHURCH

Juridical societies are not the only goal of moral reason in this world, for not even the best juridical arrangements can totally

satisfy the requirements of moral reason. Civil laws cannot address our inner duties of virtue, namely, ethical motivation
(acting from the motive of duty) and ethical ends (positively
respecting all persons). Any effort to coerce our inner duties
would be not only futile but also self-contradictory, trampling
on autonomy in the name of autonomy. Kant saw only one
hope for widespread success in promoting the spread of moral
virtue and in combating our propensity to unethical attitudes
and actions toward others. That hope lies with what he called
an "ethical society," a community composed of members affirming each other's worth and supporting each other's moral
striving. Without the supportive bonds of communal life, people are too prone to remain in an ethical state of nature, tempt-
ing one another to act immorally.

Because the moral law appears to us as sacred as if it
were God's will, reverence for that law, Kant wrote, leads us
to religion, which he defined as the performance of our duties as conscientiously as if they were divine commands. It is
therefore fitting that such a community be thought of as "a
people of God," with God as its sovereign, and that this otherwise invisible ethical society should take on the visible
form of a church. Thinking of God as moral ruler of this
community, Kant added, does not mean believing that ethical laws actually historically originated as commands of God,
for taking God's will to be the basis of duty would reduce
obedience to those laws to nonmoral heteronomy. Every
member must share in the headship of this church, for if we
were only subjects, with duties but no rights, we would be
denied our dignity as persons.

Kant believed that the historical churches had tended to con-
taminate the pure moral virtue of their members by trying to
induce them to perform morally legal actions out of fear of or
hope of eternal consequences. Nevertheless, he did not want
churches or their traditions to disappear, for he believed that,

purified of their errors, they would be the vehicles necessary to convey pure moral and religious faith.

Because it is based on the Law of Autonomy, the principle of universal law, the church should also be characterized by universality and eventually extend beyond all political boundaries to encompass the entire human race.

OUR FINAL DESTINY: THE HIGHEST GOOD

As we have seen, Kant held that good moral character or a good will is a unique, incomparable, unconditional, intrinsic good, far exceeding in value any other good (396).[2] Although it is our preeminent good, it is not our only good. Because we are dependent moral agents, happiness – our well-being as a whole – is also a genuine practical good for us (396, 401). We have both an objectively obligatory interest in our moral well-being or virtuous character and a subjectively unavoidable interest in our own natural well-being or happiness. As different as these two interests and their grounds are, we cannot renounce either. Therefore, Kant concluded that the complete final good for the human species, our ultimate "necessary end," consists in both our obligatory end – good moral character – and our natural end – happiness or well-being (see 396).

Those who have read only his *Foundations* may be surprised at Kant's inclusion of happiness in the final, comprehensive human good.[3] Throughout the *Foundations* he emphasized that our pursuit of happiness is the chief rival and impediment to morality and the reason why moral responsibilities appear to us in the form of duties. What he omitted in that book was his further claim that our desires and inclinations, considered in themselves, are good, even if only naturally good. This is why Kant did say there that we rightly take talents, many personality traits, various skills, and the "gifts of fortune" to be good in the sense that they all can contribute to our well-being (393–4). They are not of themselves morally bad, nor are they the cause of moral evil, which can be attributed only to our own will.

Although there frequently are conflicts between our pursuit of happiness and our moral obligations, such conflicts are a contingent and not a necessary matter.[4] When they do occur, however, the Law of Autonomy does command us both to recognize that morality and happiness are completely different kinds of goods and to resolve all conflicts between them by always subordinating our concern for happiness to the requirements of morality. Obedience to that law, therefore, is "the supreme condition" of morally permissible happiness and of our worthiness to be happy (396).

The answer, then, to the question What ought I to do? can be restated as: "Be virtuous, doing what makes you worthy to be happy."[5] The final question now needs to be asked again: If we do what we ought to do, for what may we then hope? What our moral reason insists on, Kant wrote elsewhere, is the right in justice of every human being to attain the morally permissible happiness each deserves. Happiness originally is a conditional and subjective end; that is, we all want to be happy but what we think will make us happy depends on our subjective desires. Once it has been sanctioned by the moral law, however, our happiness not only is tolerated as morally permissible but, what is much stronger, is commanded as part of our total final good (438–9).

The same moral law that commands us categorically to act dutifully also identifies the ultimate kingdom of ends as the consequence of dutiful actions: the human race as a collective whole must achieve its moral destiny in that kingdom in which everyone follows the moral law and each person has the happiness each deserves.[6] The existence of that kingdom is *required* by moral reason. It would be self-contradictory, Kant wrote, for our reason to command us to strive toward what is not possible; were it to do so, *all* the moral commands of reason would be thrown into doubt. We therefore *must believe* that kingdom will come to pass.

As we know, however, the demands of justice are often not served in this world; acting conscientiously does not guarantee that we will be happy. Moreover, even if we ourselves obey the moral law, we cannot count on everyone else doing so. What are the conditions required to make the *possibility* of the final highest good actual? As Kant saw it, the attainment of the kingdom of ends in its third, fullest, and most perfect form – universal happiness following upon universal obedience to the moral law – requires both a future life and the intervention of a just God who will ensure and guarantee this endeavor.

Reason, Kant argued, therefore supports what in another work, his *Critique of Practical Reason,* he called the "postulates" of immortality and of God. For our necessary moral purposes, he held, we may have a rational hope and a practical faith in the reality of the conditions necessary for the human race to achieve its moral destiny in the final kingdom of ends.

Kant insisted that this belief is part and parcel of our moral life. Were we to deny what our moral reason postulates as our moral goal and the conditions necessary for that goal, we would involve ourselves in what he called "a practical absurdity." Consistency should then require us to regard the moral law itself as an "empty figment"; yet the moral law would still be present in our moral awareness, independently of any postulates, and it would still command our absolute obedience, including our duty to contribute to the highest good.

Although Kant called this a "moral argument" for our immortality and for the existence of God, he did not claim that it is an objective proof of either; that is, he did not think it would constitute an overwhelming proof to a skeptic. But he did think it would show those who already acknowledge their moral vocation that they have a good, if subjective, reason to believe in God and to hope for the final kingdom of God.[7]

NOTES

1. Introducing Kant's ethical theory through his political theory, as I have done in this book, does not violate his injunction here, for, as we have seen, his political theory is itself based on a limited use of the first formula of the Categorical Imperative.

2. In his later writings, Kant reserved the term the "highest good" (which he used to describe the good will in *Foundations*, 396) for our total final good, and he called virtue the "supreme good." For this reason some translations of the *Foundations*, like that by Lewis White Beck, omit the phrase altogether.

3. Kant has often been misinterpreted as having held that there is only one good, namely, moral virtue, and as having had no regard at all for human needs and desires. But he did not try to argue for a moral theory that would rule happiness out of a morally good life (393, 396). In fact he elsewhere characterized such a view of morality as "misanthropic," stating that the contention that the virtuous person should not give happiness any consideration whatsoever, even when happiness is compatible with duty, completely contradicted his actual view.

4. Moral rules and prudential rules do not contradict each other, for the former tell us how to act virtuously and the latter tell us how to get what we want (424). Each is correct by its own criterion even when each recommends a course of action incompatible with the other. When there is opposition, it is between our two different interests: our interest in morality, based on reason alone, and our interest in happiness, based on desires.

5. Kant therefore held that moral philosophy may be described as a doctrine of how we are to be *worthy* of happiness (393). But that does not mean that it recommends moral character as a means to achieve happiness.

6. It is not at all clear how such different notions as virtue and happiness can be dealt with in proportional terms, and we should not expect to have any insight into matters so completely outside our experience. For example, if we try to make sense of the notion of eternity, we find ourselves thinking of a duration without time and change, and then eternity seems like a thoughtlessness that would be equivalent to annihilation. Kant himself occasionally speculated about what life after death might be like, but he concluded that for moral purposes, we can be quite indifferent about how it will work out – whether, for example, we shall live as pure spirits after death

or whether our personal identity requires the same matter that now forms our body.

7. Not everyone is impressed by Kant's "moral argument" for the existence of God and immortality. His critics grant that Kant was right in recognizing that we do think a morally good person deserves to be happy. But they also argue that this does not show that everyone really will get the happiness they deserve or that believing they actually will is necessary to morality. They argue that we could know that the highest good is attainable only if we could know on independent grounds that there is a God who guarantees its achievement. Kant held that there were no independent grounds.

6

THE LIMITS OF
THE CATEGORICAL IMPERATIVE

READERS of the *Foundations* often come to believe that Kant's moral theory is supposed to determine by itself exactly what we should or should not do. This is a deep error. However right Kant's analysis of the ultimate moral law may be, the Categorical Imperative does *not* offer us a recipe or formula for making our specific moral decisions. What it does offer are principles of great generality that either serve as negative boundaries or set out very general positive guidelines.

To put this point another way, Kant did *not* hold that living a morally good life consists in a blind adherence to absolute rules. Some passages in the *Foundations* may give the impression that he thought that morality consists only in adopting and following moral rules (see, e.g., 412–13); and, as we saw in the first chapter, he did think we need to define our public moral life in a system of public laws. But he also insisted that making the connection between general principles and individual moral decisions always requires judgments that cannot be reduced to a schematized rule-bound procedure (389). And this is what we should expect, for his respect for the subtlety of ordinary moral consciousness (391, 404) could hardly have led him to develop a moral theory that would reduce autonomous moral judgment to a mindless following of moral formulas.

In fact, in his essay "What Is Enlightenment?" he attacked mechanical rule following as diametrically *opposed to* the Enlightenment ideal that each person should act autonomously: "Rules and formulas, those mechanical aids to the rational use, or rather misuse, of his natural gifts, are the shackles of a permanent immaturity." This, he continued, is the very antithesis of our having "a rational appreciation both for our own worth and for each person's calling to think for himself."

The appreciation to which Kant refers comes down to an *attitude* that should lie behind and encompass all our more specific duties. Rules cannot totally define our lives. In government and business, for example, an unjust person will always be able to find loopholes in even the most carefully stated professional or civil codes. Kant knew this, and for that reason he held that above all we need an underlying *commitment* to the moral law that will, as it were, fill in the legislative loopholes.

In Chapters 8 and 9 we will examine that commitment in more detail. For now, we will examine what the Kantian theory says about the role of rules in our moral life.

PERMISSIBLE ACTIONS

Because Kant stressed the concept of "moral obligation," we may be tempted to think that any maxim that does *not* violate the norm of universality or of respect for persons should be understood as morally obligatory. This is far too harsh a view, and Kant's actual position again reflects his respect for ordinary moral thinking. As he saw it, strict obligation arises only negatively. The fact that a maxim does not conflict with the Categorical Imperative, then, is a sufficient condition for holding that an action based on that maxim is *permissible* and therefore is "fit" to be or "qualifies" as a *possible* maxim in an ideal moral world. An action "that does not agree with [the Categorical Imperative] is *forbidden*," whereas "an action that is compatible with the autonomy of the will is *permitted*" (439).

Because actions that are neither forbidden nor mandated are permitted, the choice of such actions, taken in isolation from other considerations, is morally arbitrary. All other things being equal, once we judge that a maxim is not morally forbidden and so also does not have a corresponding positive obligation, we have what Kant called a "moral title" either to act on or not to act on that maxim in the pursuit of our morally permissible well-being.

The fact of the matter is that most of the choices we make in our everyday lives turn out to be morally permissible ways of promoting our morally legitimate welfare and well-being. At any given moment there may be and usually are an indefinitely large number of permissible maxims on which we may act, giving us what Kant called moral "play room." Again we see how he thought that a moral theory should reflect what he called "common and everyday responsibility," here by guarding against what he called the "fanaticism" of seeing duties everywhere when in fact there are many "morally free" choices.

In the matter of permissible actions, the Categorical Imperative plays only one further role. Since we may act only on maxims that everyone else may adopt, all other things being equal, what is morally permissible for one person is also morally permissible for everyone else similarly situated.

POSITIVE DUTIES

We have repeatedly seen that Kant held that the Categorical Imperative is fundamentally a negative norm for maxims of actions, and that the most precise way to state the notion of moral obligation is to put it negatively: our fundamental maxims must not conflict with the requirement that they can serve as laws for everyone; that is, they must not fail the test of universal law. Negative duties specify what is morally forbidden and require us to limit our pursuit of happiness by the demands of morality. Kant described negative duties as narrow, strict, rigorous, and perfect, for *any* action violating them is morally wrong (421n, 424). We may never, for example, violate the respect owed another person, regardless of the reasons we may have for wanting to do so.

Stated as rules, however, our negative duties (E, or universal negative judgments in the Aristotelian Square of Opposition) also have corresponding positive duties (I, or particular positive judgments – the contradictories of E judgments). Positive duties also obligate us absolutely – just as seriously as negative duties. We may not be indifferent to or ignore them, for eventually we would have to contradict the maxim allowing everyone to ignore them (423–4). Yet Kant described them as wide, limited, and imperfect obligations (424).

Kant's point was this: rather than requiring us to perform any particular actions, in the matter of wide duties the Categorical Imperative directs us only to adopt *general* maxims, or *policies*. Beyond that, it is indeterminate in the sense of not specifying what we must do to fulfill them, or when or how.[1] (Even negative obligations do not prescribe exactly how a person should behave, but positive duties allow us much more leeway.) The prohibition against lying that we examined in Chapter 3, for example, involves a corresponding maxim of truth telling, that is, a maxim (this may sound unacceptable on first reading) to tell the truth but only to *some* people *some* of the time. Because it imposes a positive, rather than negative, duty, that maxim allows us a good deal of discretion and prudence in deciding when and to whom to tell the truth, as long as we do not violate the constraint against lying.

Unlike prohibitions, positive maxims also allow us what we might call some "vacation time"; on those occasions when we judge we are bound only by positive obligations, we are often free to simply do what we want to do, as long as we are committed to acting on those maxims later.

Kant's thinking here reflects our ordinary moral judgments: There are all sorts of ways in which we can fulfill, say, our moral obligation to develop our talents, and we are not required to devote every available moment to that task. So once again we have considerable leeway, this time in our decisions about how and how often to fulfill positive duties; and the more general the duty, the more arbitrary is our decision to obey it in one way rather than another. Because this is the case, no moral theory can determine ahead of time exactly how everyone should interpret their wide duties, and Kant did not try to offer any procedures for judgment. He did point out that if we were to try to rely on some further maxim to help us apply a particular maxim to a particular case, we would then need still another maxim for using that maxim, and so on ad infinitum. Moreover, each new maxim would still require the exercise of judgment. There simply is no substitute for the exercise of judgment.

Even if we cannot rely on *moral* principles for precise procedural guidance, we still need to live our lives as rationally as possible. The moral law remains the ultimate law of practical rationality; and it does not give us permission to make careless, stupid, or precipitous judgments. However, the only kind of rationality available to guide our judgments about how to fulfill our positive obligations is prudence, and so Kant held that such judgments both may and should be made according to *prudential* guidelines. To make our decisions as rationally as possible, we must now take into account the circumstances in which we find ourselves – how seriously, for example, someone may be in need – as well as the possible consequences of different courses of actions.

In all our decisions about positive duties, then, the moral law continues to play two important *background* roles. We have a duty to be as thoughtful as is appropriate when making those judgments that must rely on prudential considerations. And, of course, our decisions must all still be made within morally permissible parameters. For example, as we have seen, help should not be given others in a way that denigrates them.

Kant's doctrine concerning the moral indeterminacy of positive duties shows why two interpretations of the universality requirement in his moral theory are badly mistaken. The first error consists in thinking that the Categorical Imperative *always* mandates a radical impartiality, requiring us to do for everyone whatever we do for one or only some. According to this mistaken view, for example, it would be immoral for educators to give special enrichment courses to students with exceptional mental abilities. The second error holds that the Categorical Imperative requires each of us to do only and exactly what everyone else should and can do. Supposedly it would then be immoral for anyone to practice, say, almsgiving, if not everyone could do so.

But Kant again reflects common sense and holds that in the matter of positive duties we are obligated only to adopt a *policy*, say, of beneficence. People with few financial resources still can fulfill their obligation of benevolence by giving their time and talents; and what each person should do must be left to the judgment of the individual. We may all be obligated by the same positive moral policies, but those policies do not require us always to observe the criterion of universality.

CONFLICTS BETWEEN MORAL RULES

Because Kant believed that the most crucial moral conflicts occur between duty and inclination, those are the conflicts with which he is mainly preoccupied. But there can be other serious conflicts that occur *within* morality, when we seem obligated by two incompatible duties. During the Vietnam War, for example, some graduate students criticized others for studying rather than marching in protest against the war. How, according to the Kantian theory, should we decide between apparently conflicting duties? One solution comes to mind immediately. Wide duties may be satisfied in any number of ways. So in the case of a conflict between two positive duties, we might simply fulfill each of them at different times or ways. If the conflict is between a narrow obligation and a wide one, perhaps we might fulfill the narrow obligation and simply look to fulfill the wide duty in another way at another time. (As we will see in a moment, this suggestion does not always hold true.)

There are times, however, when we apparently must choose between two narrow obligations. We may be able to avoid wrongly harming another person, for example, only by telling a lie. To try to claim there are no such conflicts would fly in the face of common moral experience; such a tactic would fail to account for the facts of our moral life, just as did Socrates' denial of the reality of moral weakness.

Kant did confront this problem but only once and then only in a very summary fashion. Morality is based on reason, and reason cannot impose practical contradictions (a self-contradictory conjunction of duties). Therefore, he argued that, even when there is a conflict between moral *rules,* at any given moment we can have *only one duty.* A genuine conflict between *duties,* a conflict such that we have a duty to try to act at the same time on incompatible rules, cannot arise. "Two conflicting rules cannot both be necessary at the same time," he wrote; "if it is our duty to act according to one of these rules, then to act according to the opposite one is not our duty and is even contrary to our duty." Therefore, he continued, it is not correct to say either that our *duties* can admit of exceptions or that one *duty* can be more pressing or more obligatory than another; *all* moral obligations are *absolute.* (As we have just seen, even wide obligations do not admit of exceptions, only of a wide range of ways to fulfill them.)

When our moral rules conflict, Kant held that there can be only one (what he called) "ground of obligation" actually binding us, to be found either in the agent or in the moral rule itself. The stronger ground of, or basis for, an obligation prevails, and then "it is not only not a duty but contrary to duty to act according to the other rule." So, for example, in his political theory, Kant took the ground of the obligation to civil obedience to be at times so strong as to override many of our other moral rules, such as our direct obligation to safeguard our own life and our indirect duty to secure our own happiness.

Perhaps an analogy may help make Kant's point clearer (although he did not himself use it). We have seen how Kant likened the laws of the moral world to the laws of the natural world: they both hold universally and without exception. When a bird takes wing, its flight is not an *exception* to the law of gravity; that law still holds. The bird's flight is possible because other natural laws override the law of gravity by giving "lift" to the bird's wings. Similarly, in the case of conflicting rules, following the one with the stronger ground does not constitute following an exception to the other, which still obligates us but is overridden on this occasion.

It is unfortunate that Kant did not discuss these issues in more detail, but what he clearly had in mind is the ineluctable role of judgment in the application of moral rules. Good judgment tells us, for example, that we do not have a moral obligation actually to *act* on every moral rule at every given moment. When, for example, a teacher is dutifully preparing for his or her classes, the moral injunction against injustice still holds, but in the absence of other considerations, there is no necessity, no apparent ground of obligation, to obey that rule at that moment.

Imagine the case of a person who seems to be obligated to perform two different actions simultaneously by the same moral rule of intending to keep one's promises. She has promised to meet another person, fully intending to do so, but finds out, just before the appointed time, that her husband has had a heart attack and has been taken to the hospital. Unless there are other morally contravening considerations, clearly she is entitled to judge that her prior marriage vows have such moral weight that *her sole* obligation *at that moment* is to her spouse. When she acts on that decision, she is doing everything she is obligated to do. She may *regret* having to reschedule the appointment, but she need not feel morally *guilty* about it. The other party to the appointment may feel irritated at being inconvenienced, but he in turn has no good reason to judge her to be morally blameworthy.

In this case, the ground of obligation cannot be found simply in the rule of promise keeping, because by itself that rule would require two incompatible courses of conduct. The ground of obligation taking precedence in this case lies in the special contractual obligations undertaken by marriage partners, together with the relevant fact that one partner has a serious and urgent need for the other. This case also shows how, in our ordinary moral judgments, we do seem to reflect Kant's contention that even when our moral *rules* conflict, we do not for that reason also have conflicts between our moral *duties*. In this case, the woman does not say she made an *exception* to the rule of keeping one's truthful promises; she says, rather, that in this instance, under these circumstances, she was obligated to be with her husband.

Let us now consider another and perhaps more difficult case that Kant himself discussed in a brief article, "On a Supposed Right to Lie from Altruistic Motives." It is what today we might call a "desert island" type of case, because its occurrence is about as likely as being stranded on a desert island. Yet Kant's discussion has caused so much controversy that considering it in some detail is worthwhile.

In this case, a potential murderer demands information about the whereabouts of his intended victim, and it is "given" that the alternatives are limited so that the person being interrogated knows why he is being asked this question and is put in a position in which, as Kant put it, he "cannot avoid answering 'Yes' or 'No.' " When Kant considered this case, he was concerned *not* with the case itself but with the proposal that the *maxim* "We may lie when we judge the other person has no right to the truth" should be thought an acceptable moral rule.

In his rebuttal Kant argued that truthfulness that "cannot be avoided is the formal duty of an individual to everyone, however great may be the disadvantage accruing to himself or to another." So he concluded that a maxim must be rejected as immoral that would allow everyone to lie whenever they decide doing so would have good consequences.

We have seen that the test of a maxim is whether it can serve as a public law for everyone. Kant was not obviously in the wrong when he resisted the idea of a public law that would permit and even mandate lying; such legislation would certainly be to the advantage of Machiavellian princes and everyday manipulators. Nonetheless, Kant's view has elicited a nearly unanimous negative reaction. Given his insistence on the supreme authority of ordinary, common moral judgment, such a response is the most telling evidence that Kant's discussion was somehow flawed.

The problem is that here, as elsewhere, Kant did not clearly distinguish between judging the moral quality of a *maxim* and judging *how to act* in a particular instance. What he was arguing against was *only* the contention that a *policy* of telling lies under some circumstances is morally acceptable; as we saw in Chapter 3, he always held that a maxim permitting lying, even for "good reasons," has no place in a moral world. But most people who read Kant's discussion focus only on how they think a person should *act* in a case like this, involving a conflict between two of our usual moral rules. In this case, it would be a mistake to take the conflict to be between two rules about lying, one allowing exceptions and the other not doing so. Rather, the conflict is between a negative rule against lying and a positive rule mandating concern for the welfare of others, particularly those to whom we may have special obligations and most particularly in cases of life and death. Both these rules are grounded in respect for persons, yet in this instance we cannot observe them both. So, which rule should we judge has the stronger ground?

As we saw at the beginning of the discussion of conflicts, Kant is sometimes taken to imply that we should *always* choose a negative (narrow) obligation over a positive (wide) one. In his discussion of conflicting rules, however, he in effect denies that claim, by writing that since *all* moral obligations are absolute, we should not say that one *obligation* is more binding than another. Instead, the stronger *ground* of obligation should prevail. Since it is a requirement of reason that we not be simultaneously bound by two conflicting duties, then, in Kant's theory, once we conscientiously decide where our duty lies, the other rule is regarded as not actually obligating us here and now.

Almost everyone agrees that, in this case, the positive duty to protect another person's life, particularly a friend's life, has the stronger ground of obligation. That, therefore, is the *only* duty obligating the person in the story. In this case, then, following the negative rule against lying would in fact be, to use Kant's own words, "contrary to our duty," not because the other person has no right to the truth but because another duty temporarily overrides the usual rule. What the person being interrogated should do is to misdirect the would-be murderer.

Perhaps it may be helpful to compare Kant with Aristotle in this matter. Both held that the demands of morality are absolute, and both also acknowledged the possibility of conflicts between our usual moral rules. Kant, as we have seen, introduced the notion of the "ground of obligation" to try to deal with such conflicts. Aristotle explicitly held that the enormous complexity of human life simply makes it impossible for justice to coexist with exceptionless laws, however well they are formulated. So he introduced the notion of *epieikeia*, or "equity," to handle those exceptional cases when a good person must violate his or her normal moral code in order to do the right thing. Observing the usual rules needs no explanation, he thought, but breaking them must be justifiable on a case-by-case basis. Such justifications can be assessed against the judgments of those not personally involved in the case.

Both theories require the exercise of moral judgment, and both procedures obviously can be abused. But in neither case is obedience to our usual rules in normal situations necessarily undermined. What this discussion does indicate is that the claim that our moral rules hold absolutely needs to be interpreted very carefully.

CONFLICTING MORAL JUDGMENTS

Because conscientious compliance with the Law of Autonomy rules out the sort of subjective factors that tend to produce disagreement, Kant thought we should always be able to achieve substantial agreement on our *general* moral maxims. But this does *not* also mean that, even after the most careful public dialogues about disputed topics, everyone accepting Kant's principle will always agree about their *specific* moral judgments. There are a number of reasons for this.

For one thing, differing value systems (today often referred to as cultural diversity) can and do influence the moral thinking of most people. For example, some religions maintain that from the very beginning of conception a human fetus is a person to be respected like every other person. Others believe that in the first trimester a fetus may be a human being but should not yet be regarded as a person. There may be no satisfactory, rational way in which to resolve such differences, for, as Kant held, moral personhood is a nonempirical, nonscientific concept; in effect, he believed there are no empirical criteria for deciding who is a person. Consequently, those agreeing about the rightness of Kant's analysis of morality may still find themselves unable to reach a consensus about the morality of abortion, no matter how rational they try to be.

Again, conflicts can arise, not just between moral rules as

Kant allowed, but between competing claims, for example, to autonomy. Many cases in medical ethics involve a balancing of the claims of autonomy among all those involved: the patient, the doctors, the family, the hospital administrators, and so on. Because autonomy is not susceptible to quantified arbitration, we should not be surprised that those involved may not always be able to achieve a consensus.

Finally, although Kant himself believed in restricting the role of government mainly to protecting freedom, today most people believe that the state has a positive moral obligation to see to the welfare of all its citizens and accordingly should adopt a system of health care delivery that will fulfill that responsibility. As we have just seen, fulfilling positive duties necessarily involves prudential considerations, such as balancing various competing interests against one another. We have also seen that, partly because our resources are limited, the fulfillment of positive obligations to others does not require us to treat everyone exactly alike. Since even our nation has limited resources, decisions about health care delivery inevitably must involve trade-offs aimed at trying to achieve a balance between available resources on the one hand and all the different interests involved on the other.

In our personal associations we may often give preference to those nearest to us emotionally, but in public political decisions the use of a utilitarian decision procedure is restricted by the requirements of justice. This means, in general, that public health legislation should be constrained to use impersonal, disinterested, and impartial criteria that ignore which individuals' interests may or may not be served. As Kant saw, however, people engaging in prudential reasoning do not think it sensible to set aside consideration of their own self-interest, and everyone wants his or her interests given special consideration. As a consequence, regardless of what public decisions are made, they can and surely will be attacked as denigrating the worth of some individuals or some groups. This, as Kant would have pointed out, simply reflects the fact that reason suffers ineluctable limitations as a guide to happiness and welfare. If, as he argued, reason is not a sure guide in such matters for the individual, it clearly is even less suited to determining how to make everyone happy.

CONSCIENCE

Difficult and conflicting moral decisions also raise questions about the role and power of what we generally call our "conscience." Because an essential point of Kant's moral theorizing was to defend the inner freedom of the individual, that is, to liberate the individual person's judgment from domination by outside control, we would expect him to have emphasized the sanctity of the individual conscience. And he of course did so.

What needs to be said first is that Kant maintained that we do not have a duty to *have* a conscience; he thought that simply having a conscience is inevitable, intrinsic in our having reason, of being rational agents. But we do have a duty to cultivate it and sharpen our attentiveness to it. In Kant's analysis, conscience is the sort of moral questioning we do when we reflect on either past or possible future actions. Since, according to Kant, we cannot be certain, in even one case, of the purity of our motives and the sincerity of our intentions, in our self-examinations we are limited mainly to questioning our efforts to ensure the moral *legality* of our behavior. When we look at past actions, we can and do question whether we were sufficiently careful in determining how we ought to have acted and whether we in fact followed those determinations conscientiously. When we look to future actions, we need frequently to reaffirm our determination to do our duty, whatever it may be.

We commonly believe that people can have a misinformed conscience, but this is a judgment made from the outside. As Kant saw it, judgments of conscience, conscientiously made, *cannot* be wrong for the person making them. We can realize we are in error only when we can distinguish between what is true and what we have mistakenly believed to be true. But if there is no more ultimate moral authority than the judgment of our own practical reasoning, we cannot make such a distinction about *our own* present judgments of conscience. In *that* sense, according to Kant, an erroneous conscience is "a logical impossibility" and "nothing more can be required of" a person. If we judge, to the best of our ability, that we are making and following our moral judgments as carefully as we can, then we must regard our decisions as being as sacred as if they were divine verdicts.

Kant's doctrine may have been radical in his day but that doctrine has become so much a part of our ordinary moral thinking that almost everyone now regards the claim that a morally good person must conscientiously follow his or her convictions about what is right and wrong as simply not open to challenge.

ERRONEOUS MORAL JUDGMENTS

The emphasis that Kant placed on conscience also raises questions about how he regarded erroneous moral judgments. When we make our specific moral judgments, he wrote, no one has any access to moral principles not also available to everyone else (404). Maintaining that we have no higher moral guide than our own reason means putting the burden for moral decisions on the judgment of the individual, and that presupposes that each of us *can* judge what is right and wrong. However, our personal moral experience leads us to believe that even good people can and do make bad moral judgments and therefore act wrongly, even from the motive of duty. How frequently this happens can only be guessed, since we have no sure access to others' thinking. But there is always the possibility that in some moral matters any of us might suffer invincible ignorance, that is, be sufficiently unenlightened as not to realize that we are in error. In that sense moral enlightenment is always a process in progress.

Kant did not wish to deny that this is the case, but unfortunately he did not discuss moral errors in any detail. Given what he wrote in the *Foundations,* however, we know that he thought that all philosophers before him had been mistaken about the fundamental nature of human morality, though elsewhere he added that that by itself did not indicate they were bad people. What he did offer as our best safeguard against errors were what he called "dialectical rules" for guiding our moral judgments: (1) think for yourself; (2) think from the standpoint of every other person; and (3) think consistently. Such conditions, taken together, amount to a procedural restatement of the Law of Autonomy; and they emphasize that autonomy is not only a quality of free, rational agents but also both an impersonal and a social ideal. Correct moral judgments are most likely to emerge in the forum of open and public debate, where, particularly in difficult cases, our thinking can be tested for errors and idiosyncrasies. (Remember his political Principle of Publicity, discussed in Chapter 1.) Kant thought that all sincere moral disagreements, including those arising from different cultural and religious traditions, should be tested by these rules.[2] Given his faith in the Enlightenment, Kant seemed confident that, in the forum of public debate, reason and truth would eventually triumph.

THE VALUE OF A MORAL THEORY

We are now in a position to discuss in more detail the role and value of a moral theory. Kant offered some important suggestions about this topic in the opening pages of the *Foundations.* We saw in Chapter 2 that practical reason has three roles – critical, creative, and imperative – but moral theory has only the critical role. When we engage in moral theorizing, as we have been doing with Kant throughout this book, we reflect critically on our practical goals and formulate principles by which to live our lives. We do this, as Kant said, because we need clarity about our moral life, and achieving such clarity is exactly what he identified as the main task for and contribution of moral theorizing (405). As for the imperative role of practical reason, the knowledge we gain from moral theory does not necessarily mean that we will act rightly; we still need to make an ultimate commitment to the moral law. Finally, the creative role of practical reason consists in deciding specific moral questions; and nowhere did Kant indicate that the purpose of a moral theory is to tell people exactly what they should or should not do.

Kant further held that there are no moral experts in the sense of some few people possessing some special, privileged information that enables them to make better, more accurate moral judgments than others. When making particular moral judgments about how to act, ordinary people "have as much hope as any philosopher of hitting the mark" (404). They do not need to be taught anything new (404); on the contrary, the test of a philosophical analysis of morality is its fidelity to the moral judgments of ordinary people. He did, however, allow that moral experience and informed reflection can help all of us make better judgments than we otherwise might (389).

If clarity is the main contribution of a moral theory, exactly how did Kant think a moral theory could accomplish that goal? It can discourage us from rationalizing our desires, he wrote, by clearly stating the ultimate moral norm, the Categorical Imperative, and then by showing us how to use that norm to distinguish between our quest for happiness and the requirements of morality (404–5). Here Kant used a helpful metaphor: the Categorical Imperative functions as a "moral compass" to guide us in our decision making, without determining exactly what those decisions must be (404).

Further, a moral theory can also offer us an extensive set of concepts – a vocabulary – with which to identify, organize, articulate, and discuss specific moral issues. It is not that such a theory just makes up those concepts; rather, they are initially part and parcel of what people tend to find important in their ethical discussions. Moral theorizing then tries to make their meaning more precise and their relationships to one another more coherent than is often the case in ordinary speech. In effect, it enables us to think more perceptively and make more sensitive discriminations, thereby helping us reflect more thoughtfully on our moral life.

Finally, an adequate moral theory also insists on respect for everyone involved in moral discussions.

We may be disappointed to find that moral philosophy has a more modest role than we originally had hoped. If so, we need to remember that Kant himself did not mislead us into expecting more, even though he believed that moral theorizing has a crucial contribution to make to our lives.

Lest we underestimate the help that Kant's theory can give us, let us briefly consider a problem for which no moral theory, Kant's included, can suggest a solution, at least for the present: the morality of abortion. Picture what has become a common scenario: a highly emotionally charged confrontation between two groups outside an abortion clinic. Each group engages in name calling; the anger and frustration mount; threats are exchanged, verbal and physical harassment spread at the scene; and finally the disagreement escalates to violence and then murder. Or consider another tragic scenario, this one occurring in parts of Eastern Europe where racial and religious hatred escalated to another case of "ethnic cleansing" of staggering proportions, an appalling renewal of all the horrors of the Nazi "final solution."

In a world in which violence seems to be becoming more the norm than the exception for conflict resolution, we find the world regressing to what Kant and others called "the state of nature," in which confrontational tactics and violence are the preferred way in which to deal with disputes. In such situations, political force, not reason, may be the only way in which to control the hostility between people that earlier Kant had found rampant throughout the history of the human race. This allows us the two possibilities we have already mentioned: a tyranny, a leviathan like the one Hobbes had described, or a government having sufficient power to curb the hostility but based on respect for everyone. The latter political structure requires that the citizens exercise restraint and engage in the sort of discussions that should characterize the attempt to resolve differences reasonably within a community in which the members respect each other.

When there are apparently irreconcilable differences of moral convictions, Kant's theory can still contribute several suggestions about how to deal with the very lack of agreement. First, when it is not clear that anyone possesses the truth about the matter in dispute (no matter how certain each side is that it alone possesses the truth), no one has a moral title to hate, condemn, or persecute others with a different view. This means that a liberal society (in the sense explained in the first chapter) must work very hard at promoting tolerance for differences.[3] Second, such tolerance should be based, not on a relativism that holds there is no moral truth, but on the principle that, in such situations, each person has the obligation to hold conscientiously to his or her convictions about what is the morally correct position, *and* each person is *also* obligated to grant that everyone else has the same right. Third, no one has a moral right to threaten or coerce those with whom they disagree.

In the meantime, discussions should continue in the hope that a peace based on mutual respect can be reached. (In the case of abortion, the same sort of technical advances that helped bring about the problem may also hold promise of a solution.) As long as there is no "general will," legislators should acknowledge that that is the case, and whatever legislation they find necessary must be enacted prudently and gradually, so as not to violate the respect owed all the citizenry.

In such ways, the instruction we get from Kant's moral theory can guide great areas of our life even if it does not totally determine any of them.

NOTES

1. In 421n Kant wrote, "I understand here by a perfect duty one which allows no exception in the interests of inclination," seemingly implying that we may make exceptions to wide or imperfect duties. This was an unfortunate choice of wording, for a decision made just on the basis of personal preference, say, to donate to the cancer fund rather than to the heart fund, does not constitute an exception to the wide duty of beneficence. Elsewhere Kant amended what he had written: "A wide duty is not to be taken as a permission to make exceptions to the maxim of actions, but only as a permission to limit one maxim of duty by another."

2. In contrast, Kant wrote elsewhere that an egoist refuses "to test his judgment by the understanding of others," because he "sees no use in anything except what is personally useful to him and contributes to his own happiness, not in the thought of duty."

3. Kant discussed tolerance mainly in connection with differences in religious beliefs; when there is no objective way to arbitrate between religious differences, he wrote, there is "no such thing" as treason against God.

7

MORALITY AND PRUDENCE
(*FOUNDATIONS* 2)

S O far we have examined Kant's analysis of the role and scope of the Categorical Imperative in determining the morality of our maxims or practical policies. In this chapter, we will approach his theory of moral life from a new and different perspective, by setting out the contrast he made between morality and prudence in the second section of the *Foundations*. We will do this by first looking at his general description of our ability to direct our actions intelligently, then examining his account of prudence, and finally seeing how, in his judgment, morality is radically different from prudence. Taking this approach will give us the opportunity to consider Kant's analysis of maxims from a different focus.

PRACTICAL REASON IN GENERAL

We can relate to the world in two very different ways. We do so theoretically, as observers, when we seek only to understand the world; and we do so practically, as agents, when we try to change the world to what we want it to be or think it ought to be (387).[1] Traditionally, Western philosophy had taken our ability to reason to be *the* distinctive feature of human agency. Kant stood firmly within that tradition, and in the second section of the *Foundations* he discussed how our agency is guided by what, in his faculty psychology, he referred to, interchangeably, as "practical reason" and the "will" (412; see 446). This is the power we have to select goals in which we are interested, to form rules for achieving them, and finally to act on those rules.

Identifying goals. As Kant saw it, there are no rational actions that are completely aimless; we cannot act rationally without an end in view (387).[2] Before we begin to think about how to act, then, we first need to find a goal toward which to strive. Kant called this the end or object or "matter" of an action (460n). Since we cannot always get what we want by ourselves, we need to develop what he called the "worldly wisdom" to know how to get the help of others when we need it (416n). Even then our intentions are frequently frustrated, for the world does not guarantee that our efforts will always be successful. What we always have control over, however, are our intentions.[3]

Being interested. We have to decide that something is worth pursuing before we take an interest in it as a goal. Kant held that the notion of "having an interest in something" can never be attributed to beings lacking reason; they "merely experience sensuous impulses" (459n). In his view, one of the things that makes our agency radically different from that of animals is this very ability to select our own goals.

Acting on rules. The next function of practical reasoning (or the will) is to help us figure out how to attain our goals. When we are clear about how to do so, we should be able to articulate the conclusions of our deliberations in the form of practical rules. Since all rational actions are goal-directed, these are all "material" rules. Once we find our rules are correct, we tend to adopt them as general policies to be acted upon whenever appropriate. As we have seen, Kant called those rules we either are considering adopting or actually have adopted our "maxims" (400, 400n, 421n). We have also seen that maxims are rules of conduct having varying degrees of generality. They range from rules that are objective and hold for everyone (as do morally acceptable civil laws) to those that are merely subjective because they articulate only a single individual's intention or disposition. Either might be the appropriate answer if a person were asked the reason for acting in a particular way.

The power to adopt and act on rules of our own making has enormous importance: "Everything in nature works in accordance with laws. Only a rational being has the capacity of acting according to the *conception* of laws, that is, according to principles" (412). Of course, a rational agent who is acting in an accustomed way does not need to have a maxim explicitly in mind while acting, and people can also act nonrationally, say, impulsively, passionately, carelessly, absentmindedly, and so on. The fact that we can act nonrationally has the consequence that *all* practical rules appear to us as commands or imperatives, as rational constraints against any tendency we may have to act nonrationally (400n, 412–14).

One of Kant's main strategies in the *Foundations* for clarifying the nature of morality was to contrast two kinds of practical reasoning: moral ("pure practical") reasoning and prudential ("empirical") reasoning. He thought this comparison needed to be made because he believed that all previous philosophers had badly confused the two (390, 409–10).

PRUDENCE

If we read only the *Foundations*, we might conclude that Kant thought that our only legitimate practical interests are all moral in nature. But in that book he explicitly said that although morality is the most important practical good, it is not the only such good (396).

The goal of prudence. Kant was acutely aware that we have a wide variety of needs we must meet not only to survive but also to lend some quality to our lives. Consequently, he thought our welfare is second in importance only to our moral vocation, and he argued that we have an inescapable responsibility and right to be concerned about what seems to us in

116

our own best interest (415). The term he generally used to refer to our well-being as rational but finite beings was "happiness," which included the satisfaction of our needs and desires as a whole, our enjoyment of and contentment with such a fulfilled life, and a reasonable confidence in its continuance (393, 405, 416, 418).

Kant decided that for his purposes in the *Foundations* it would be sufficient to analyze the goal of prudence in hedonistic terms, with happiness taken as consisting simply in attaining pleasure and avoiding pain. Pleasure is the enjoyable feeling we get when our life is prospering, and we feel pain when our desires are being frustrated. From experience, he added, we learn that choosing one pleasure often means giving up another and that happiness as a whole may require us to give up some individual pleasures we still really want. So we have to learn to frustrate some desires and "tame" others. The ability to do so, he wrote, is the meaning of prudence in the sense of "personal wisdom" (416n).

We clearly need to try to determine what we think will contribute to our happiness. Once again, if we read only the *Foundations*, we might conclude that Kant thought we would be better off if we never worried about such things. When we concern ourselves with what we want, he wrote, we only tend to multiply our desires; and because we cannot satisfy them all, we easily end up less, not more, happy (395–6). Further, when we try to imagine what will make us happy, we find that no matter how thoughtful we may be, we still cannot form a definite, firm, and consistent notion of happiness for ourselves, much less for others (399, 418). Our desires seem to resist our best efforts to devise a sort of calculus of satisfactions. So, he concluded, prudential reasoning turns out to be a singularly weak guide to happiness; it cannot hope to offer us reliable maxims for the attainment of a goal upon which it cannot focus clearly (395, 399).

Such passages in the *Foundations*, however, do not accurately represent Kant's complete view of the matter, for in that book he exaggerated the limitations of prudential planning in order to point up the superiority of moral interests and the power of moral reasoning. In other works he clearly held that we are well advised to seek what is in our best interest; in such matters we should not rely just on luck.

Prudential interest. Our inclinations always provide the motive for prudential behavior; we act only because we want something or other.[4] But this is not to say that we are compelled by our desires; it is up to us whether or not we act on them. If, for example, we have competing desires, then we need to decide what we want most. But when we do act, we act *out of* our interest in whatever it is that we want. Kant called this an "interest of inclination." In such cases we have only a "mediate interest" in the action itself; what we care about is not the action itself but what acting will get us (460n).

Prudential imperatives. Once we have decided what we want, we need to figure out how to get it (413n, 414–16). Kant called this use of reason "empirically conditioned," for it is only from experience that we learn both what we want and how to get it. The rules we then formulate are "right" insofar as they are effective (415).

All particular prudential maxims presuppose and instantiate the same general principle of self-love or happiness: insofar as you are rational, genuinely wanting an end also means willing whatever means (you know) are available and necessary to get it. This principle is analytically true, Kant wrote, following from an analysis of what it means to be an agent with desires who acts rationally to satisfy them (417, 419).[5]

Because we do not always act rationally even in matters of self-interest, both the ultimate prudential rule and all the more specific prudential rules appear to us in the form of *imperatives* (414). But they also bind us only *hypothetically,* because they all presuppose what Kant described as "a subjective and contingent condition": the provision that we want the specified ends (416; see 414–18). All prudential imperatives at least implicitly have the following conditional form: If you genuinely want x (this end), then (you ought to) do y (the means to that end). Rationally, we then have only two choices: to adopt the means or to give up the end.

Because we can desire an almost limitless number of different things, an indefinitely large number of such imperatives are possible (414–15). They can all be grouped, however, into two classes, because the ends to which they are relevant are all of two general kinds. In the case of things or states of affairs that we may or may not want, Kant calls the rules for attaining them "technical rules" and "rules of skill," for they all involve knowledge of causal connections in the world (414–16).[6] The second type of imperative concerns happiness as an end, something we may presume everyone wants. In the *Foundations*, Kant calls the rules for pursuing happiness "assertoric," "pragmatic," and, most commonly, "prudential" rules (using "prudential" in a more restricted sense here) (415). Let us look at each of these two kinds of rules in turn.

Imperatives of skill. Technical principles describe how the physical world works; we learn them through experience, and when they are correct, they are theoretical statements that hold objectively, for everyone. What makes such knowledge practically relevant to us so we use it to guide our actions is something else, namely, our desires for whatever that information will help us get. Then, for example, the theoretical statement "Water boils at 212°F at sea level" becomes the practical and hypothetical imperative "If you want to boil water at sea level, raise its temperature to 212°F." Introducing desires to make it a practical rule means the loss of its objectivity; it becomes only subjectively valid, holding only contingently, only for those people who have the relevant desires and aims. We can disregard these kinds of imperatives any time we wish – whenever we decide not to pursue the relevant goal because, for example, the cost of trying to reach it is just too high (413, 420).

Imperatives of happiness. Even though happiness is something that everyone necessarily wants, Kant argued that prudential imperatives (in the narrow sense of imperatives of happiness) also hold only contingently and hypothetically (416, 418–19). In fact, he held that they are even more subjective than technical imperatives (which they may contain), so much so that he preferred not to call them rules at all, but only counsels. We already have seen one of his reasons for doing so: happiness is an idea of the imagination that refuses to stay in sharp focus. Moreover, different people count different things as part of their happiness, so that the same imperatives do not hold for everyone (417). Further, the pursuit of happiness often depends on circumstances that are as fluid as our desires, so that even the best prudential rules hold only for the most part and must allow for exceptions (417–18).

Of course, we do have common needs, so that we often find ourselves wanting the same things as other people. But since those things that happen to be widely desired are also for that reason often in short supply, shared wants often lead to enormous conflict rather than to happiness.

Kant's conclusion was that we have no principle for deciding how to attain any lasting happiness in this world. Even the best prudential rules are at best only counsels or pieces of advice that hold only for the most part (418–19). They turn out to say something like this: If you happen to count such and such as part of what will make you happy, then many people have found this a good rule to follow. Of course, your situation may be somewhat different, and you may not want to follow this rule if doing so excludes other things you happen to count as part of your well-being. So this particular rule is only advice that you might want to consider but that you also might decide to reject. Whichever way you act, your decision could still turn out badly. Or it could turn out much better than you had hoped. There is no way to know ahead of time.

CONTRASTING PRUDENCE AND MORALITY

When Kant criticized the analyses of other philosophers in the second section of the *Foundations* (406–10), he allowed that they had begun correctly when they held that, before we act, we must first take an interest in acting. But then they incorrectly presumed that we can take an interest only in what we want; nothing can be considered good unless it first is desired (432–3). So they concluded that the only way to discover what is morally good is to inventory and classify all the various things that people have desired. The "best" or "highest" or "noblest," whether it be pleasure or conformity to societal standards, to some ideal of perfection, or to the will of God, should be given the honorific title of "morally good"; and then those actions will be morally right that promote that good (441–3).

The blunder of claiming that we can be moved to act only by something lying outside our reason, Kant argued, led them to identify morality with *heteronomy*, with being "other-lawed" (443). If their analyses were correct – if Hume was right in holding that our practical reasoning can only play the role of servant to our desires – then all our practical rules can only be hypothetical rules, and there can be no such thing as morality as we commonly think of it, with categorical laws (444). In effect, those philosophers ended up not with a moral theory but merely with a psychosociological study, an "empirical anthropology" of human hopes and fears (390–1). By contrast, the most fundamental requirement of morality is *autonomy*, that is, the power of reason to enact laws, to be "a law unto itself," regardless of any influences from outside itself (440).

When examining both the political Principle of Law and the moral Law of Autonomy, we saw that Kant drew his analysis of morality from "ordinary moral consciousness," that is, from what and how ordinary people think when they think about moral matters. The contrasts he drew between morality and prudence also depend on the same moral convictions of ordinary people.

Contrasting their respective interests. Because our inclinations aim only at attaining pleasure and avoiding pain, they can just as easily lead either to moral or to immoral actions, depending on what promises pleasure or threatens pain (390, 398, 442). Desires, therefore, cannot function as a reliable basis for moral decisions, which often require their frustration rather than their fulfillment. Further, moral goodness or the lack of it is an attribute of a person's intentions, or will. Desires, therefore, are neither morally good nor evil; they simply lack intrinsic moral significance or worth.

To review very briefly, the moral law commands our obedience unconditionally, without relying on any desires or inclinations we might have. As a consequence, we must be able to act on the basis of our own reason alone, without relying on other incentives. As we shall see in the next chapter, our reason by itself must be able to generate an immediate and practically efficacious interest *in* acting dutifully, without our acting *from* any interests based on our inclinations (413n, 441, 444, 449, 460).

Contrasting their respective imperatives. Kant offered two main criticisms of prudential rules. First, they hold only subjectively and contingently – only when we have desires they can help satisfy. If we have no relevant desires or if we give up trying to satisfy relevant desires, we are free to ignore prudential rules (420, 426–8, 442, 444). Second, because they represent possible actions as good only as *means,* the actions they recommend are only instrumentally good (427–8).

According to common moral thought, however, moral imperatives bind us objectively and necessarily as rational beings; we are never free to ignore them (389, 402–3, 411–13, 420–1, 426–7, 440). Moreover, as the test of the Categorical Imperative shows, moral rightness is an intrinsic quality of intentions and does not depend on whether or not they will promote our advantage (402–3, 413n, 414–16, 441, 444, 460n). Consequently, prudential rules are not fit to serve as moral rules, and prudential actions have no intrinsic moral worth.[7]

Contrasting their respective ends. It is true that we regard happiness, like moral goodness, as an intrinsic good; we pursue it for its own sake, not as an instrumentality. But in our ordinary judgments we also are convinced that happiness and morality are two entirely different things (442). We may be pleased, for example, to see others happy, but we do not think they are by that fact also morally good. We also know people can be very unhappy even when they are morally good, as well as happy even if they have not been morally good (393). Moreover, as Kant pointed out very early in the *Foundations,* happiness can lead to pride and arrogance; rather than being identifiable with morality, happiness always is in need of moral constraints.

Similar remarks can be made about all of the mental, psychological, and physical assets that can help a person to be happy and that Kant listed in the first section of the *Foundations* (393–4). The fact that superior talents of one sort or another may enable us to charge more for our time and services simply shows that such qualities have only instrumental worth. Like happiness itself, they are also only conditionally good, for they can contribute to either morally good or morally evil purposes; and their use in the pursuit of happiness is also subject to restraints imposed by morality.[8]

By contrast, as we have seen, the value of virtuous character, of a good will, does not depend on anything outside itself, nor can it be misused. It alone is always intrinsically good, without qualification (393–5).

Conclusion. Kant concluded that it is a deep error to equate prudence with morality. There is nothing about prudence that gives us any reason to think that it has any intrinsic *moral* significance whatsoever (441–2).

A NONEMPIRICAL BASIS FOR MORALITY

Why then did so many previous thinkers fall into the same mistake of confusing morality and happiness? Kant's view was that they did so because, from Aristotle to Machiavelli to Hume, they all had based their analysis of morality on experience. This is a capital blunder, because learning what people in fact *do* tells us nothing about what they *ought* to do (407–8). On the basis of experience we can learn only contingent facts about human beings and their lives; and such generalities can offer us only hypothetical maxims that are not fit to serve as the basis for the absolute and universal manner in which the laws of morality appear to us (389, 406–9, 425–8, 431, 442, 444). Further, experience cannot offer us even one sure example of specifically moral motivation (406–7); in fact, empirical studies like psychology regard all human actions as caused by prior, nonmoral desires. So if we were to try to base morality on experience, we would have to conclude that there is no evidence for any specifically moral motivation (407–8, 419). Moreover, morality commands actions we may never have encountered in experience, like true friendship (407–8).

All these considerations mean that previous philosophers could not possibly have understood the nature of morality correctly (390, 409–11). Their methodology ruled out the very possibility of a *categorical* imperative and with it morality itself. In effect, by condemning hedonism, Kant also refuted its modern counterpart, Utilitarianism, long before John Stuart Mill was born.

THE POWER OF MORAL REASON

From his analysis of the categorical manner in which moral principles obligate us, Kant concluded that they cannot be based on an appeal to desires but must be based only on what he called "pure practical reason" (he did not use the expression "moral reason" himself) (432–3). That is why he maintained that moral laws hold, not just for human beings, but for all rational beings and for human beings only because they are rational (389, 425). Therefore, as a cognitive power, pure practical reason must enable us to identify ends that are objectively good, that is, necessarily good for everyone, independently of all subjective desires and aversions (396, 413–14, 427, 431–3). It must also be able to identify, through the Categorical Imperative, maxims that are right, independently of any consideration of possibly adverse consequences of following those maxims.

So that we will take an interest in and care about morality, pure practical reason must also be a conative power, by itself able to arouse in us sufficient interest in acting morally so that we will be motivated to act on its judgments, frustrating, when necessary, any opposition from our desires (400–1, 460). This interest, Kant wrote, is "nonsensuous," for it is based, not on the anticipation of any pleasure, but on our prior recognition of the moral law within us and on the *respect* that recognition generates. The moral law "is not valid for us because it interests us . . . it interests us because it is valid for us," based as it is on our own reason (460–1). As we shall see in Chapter 8, respect and other specifically moral emotions play a crucial role in human moral life.

FREEDOM AND AUTONOMY

All this constitutes what has been called Kant's "Copernican revolution" in moral philosophy. No one before him had suggested that human reason could be so powerful a cognitive and conative power, enabling us to judge and act autonomously, that is, in a completely "self-lawed" fashion (446–7). To attribute such power to us is also to attribute to us an equally radical freedom. Such freedom has both negative and positive aspects. Negatively, we are not bound by the causal laws that heteronomously dominate the world of nature; when we deliberate and act, we are *free from* determination by any prior or concurrent causes outside and alien to our own reason. Positively, we have the power of absolute self-determination; we are *free to* act as "first causes," to exercise causal power spontaneously, solely on the basis of standards or principles given by our own reason (412). Kant thereby attributed to us a deeper freedom than anyone before him had thought possible (and many after him, too) (446–7).

In his discussion of freedom at the beginning of the third section of the *Foundations,* Kant pointed out that the notion of causality presupposes that all changes in the world occur in a law-governed way, so that they are all the effects of appropriate causes. The fact that we are free in the negative sense from such laws of nature does not mean that we may now act in a lawless fashion. To the contrary, the world of freedom and morality has its own law, the law of rational self-determination, the Law of Autonomy. A radically free will is one that acts only on general maxims that can at the same time be laws for all other free wills. Thus, Kant concluded, "a free will and a will under moral laws are identical" (447).

In our ordinary way of speaking, we often take freedom to be what Kant called "psychological freedom," that is, the absence of both internal and external impediments to doing what we *want* to do. In his political writings Kant himself tended to use the word "freedom" in this sense. But for the purposes of ethics he held that such an understanding of freedom is completely inadequate, for it allows us, at best, only prudential, not morally significant, conduct.

Today the term "autonomy" is often used not only as a moral but also as a psychological "pro-word." In the humanistic theories of Abraham Maslow, Carl Rogers, and Lawrence Kohlberg, for example, it is used to designate the psychological ideal of a mature – a "self-actualizing" or "fully functioning" – self-directed person. In those theories, however, the term tends to function more like Kant's principle of prudence than as his law of morality, since the emphasis is placed on individual recognition of ourselves as unique complexes of needs and desires.

"Autonomy" is also used today to refer to what is often regarded as an absolute *right* (variously identified as psychological, legal, and/or moral) of persons to make their own decisions and to control their own lives without interference by others. Today the term "autonomy" has such powerful connotations that it often is used as an "argument-stopper"; to accuse someone of not respecting another's right of autonomy is to condemn the first person's actions as wrong – often as morally wrong.

By contrast, persons described as lacking autonomy are called "heteronomous" in the sense of being excessively other-directed. They are described as uncritically willing to shape their feelings and behaviors so as to conform to the expectations of others, whoever or whatever the "others" may be: one's parents, one's peers or social group, or political or ecclesiastical authority.

These contemporary uses of "autonomy" do bear some resemblance to their Kantian ancestor, for, like Kant's notion, they require the exercise of practical reasoning. They also reflect the conviction that the autonomous person can and should be responsible, that is, self-governing; and further, they rule out certain kinds of coercive interference by others. But here the similarities end, for Kant's ideas of "autonomy" and "heteronomy" are far more precise and restricted than the contemporary notions.

For Kant the term "autonomy" denoted our ability and responsibility to know what *morality* requires of us and to act accordingly. In a derivative sense, the autonomous person is one who exercises this ability and lives up to this responsibility.[9] Rather than being a norm for promoting and satisfying our desires, then, the Law of Autonomy functions fundamentally as "the supreme limiting condition of all subjective ends," whatever they may be (431). It is just the fact that morally right maxims qualify as universal laws that shows that they are not and cannot be essentially self-seeking.

There are also similarities between Kant's and present-day notions of heteronomy: A person is heteronomous who is other-directed. But thinkers today tend to define "others" as other persons or institutions, whereas Kant regarded *anything* outside our own reason as "other." To choose to follow one's own desires rather than one's reason is, for Kant, the paradigm of heteronomous behavior. A person will only conform to the norms and expectations of others if he or she yields to a desire to do so, either because doing so will contribute to his or her well-being or because not doing so will endanger that same well-being.

As we saw in Chapter 1, our obligations toward others are not based on their rights; rather, their rights are based on our prior obligations. The consequence is that Kant regarded autonomy as, most fundamentally, an ability and an obligation providing the only possible basis for both moral and political rights.

NOTES

1. In these introductory remarks the term "practical" is used to refer to both prudential and moral activity in contrast to theoretical activity. In the *Foundations*, however, Kant usually meant the term "practical" to be synonymous with "moral" and to contrast with "prudential" (e.g., 399, 406, 412).
2. We saw, when examining the Categorical Imperative, that the morality of an action is not based on goals or ends of any kind. Kant's

manner of stating that claim occasionally is misread to mean that we can only act morally rightly if we act without *any* end in view.

3. This claim is very important, since, as we have seen, in Kant's theory moral "actions" refer primarily to intentions and only secondarily to physical behaviors following those intentions. (Today some philosophers would disagree with Kant, holding that intentions are not internal actions but states of mind.) Consequently, when, in the *Foundations,* Kant described *actions* performed from duty and for the sake of duty (therefore including the agent's motive and intended end) as having moral worth, he was in fact describing the moral quality of the *agents* having such intentions.

4. Kant's calling our desires "pathological" was not meant to imply they are somehow diseased or perverse (413n). He intended this to mean only that they are the sort of psychophysical phenomena that psychologists use to explain our actions.

5. The ultimate principle of prudence is an objective principle that holds for all rational beings with desires; by contrast, the moral law holds for everyone just as a rational agent. As a consequence, *individual* prudential maxims can hold only subjectively, that is, only if they serve a particular person's desires, but the basic moral maxims hold objectively, for everyone, regardless of anyone's desires.

6. In 414–15 of the *Foundations* Kant also called rules of skill "problematic imperatives," because it is only possible and in that sense problematic that we will want the ends to which they are relevant. Later he decided that the notion of a "possible imperative" is incoherent; every imperative commands an action, even if it does so only conditionally.

7. The *rules* generated by the two uses of reason do not conflict with each other; the rivalry is between our prudential and moral interests.

8. Kant was careless when he described the various natural goods as "bad and harmful" when they are not used in morally right ways (393–4); only *persons* can be morally good or bad.

9. Kant was indebted here both to the Stoics, who had characterized the virtuous man as having autonomy, and to Rousseau, who had suggested the meaning of autonomy to Kant when, in his *Social Contract,* he had written: "Obedience to a law which one has prescribed to himself is freedom." Rousseau was preoccupied, as was Kant, with protecting freedom within the authoritative structure of the state.

8

MORAL CHARACTER

WE can discuss the nature of character from either a theoretical or a practical point of view. From the theoretical, or empirical, point of view, that typically taken in the social sciences, we think of a person's character as consisting of inherited qualities modified by acquired habits and a wide variety of external influences such as family and education. From this point of view, we regard a person's character as completely explicable in terms of prior causal factors. Having admirable character traits, for example, may simply be a result of the right natural emotional inheritance together with good parenting and a supportive environment. If we could know all such influences, we should be able to predict exactly how a person would act in various situations.

Kant understood that anyone wanting to understand human conduct scientifically had to take the view that we, like the rest of nature, are causally determined; we can explain human behavior only if we can identify its causal antecedents. But as he also pointed out, this interpretation makes the notions of moral character and personal responsibility meaningless, for they both require that we be free, that is, able to exercise our agency without being causally determined (425–6).

We regard ourselves and the world from a practical point of view when, as agents, we think about acting or actually do so. From this point of view, we necessarily regard ourselves as free and responsible for the quality of our character. What we are depends on what *we* make of ourselves rather than on what nature and other people make of us. Not surprisingly, Kant held that, to construct a moral theory, we need to analyze our self-awareness as agents from the practical point of view.

The most prominent fact to emerge from Kant's analysis of our everyday moral consciousness is that our inner moral life is a constant struggle. We find ourselves torn between the laws of morality and the allurements of pleasure. Because we are physical beings with needs, we just naturally experience desires; and because we also are rational beings, we cannot avoid the demands of morality. Further, since we seek both unlimited happiness and merited moral self-esteem, our prudential and moral interests tend to compete with each other in what Kant characterized as an ongoing internal *dialectic* (405).[1] As a consequence, the fact that morality appears to us as our duty is most in evidence when our inclinations oppose the moral law (387, 425).

Our desires are, as Kant put it, "pathological" (somatic) events that just happen to us. They simply are. Even though we are always free to resist or ignore them, we cannot avoid being affected by them. Because our desires and aversions are not under our control, Kant wrote, in his *Metaphysics of Morals*, "I cannot [generate the feeling of] love because I *will* to, still less because I *ought* to. . . . So a *duty to love* is logically impossible." (See 399–400). It follows that just having certain desires, whether supportive of or contrary to the moral law, is neither morally praiseworthy nor morally blameworthy. Moreover, desires are all heteronomous, "other-lawed," and as we have seen, moral motivation cannot be based on heteronomy (399–401).

Desires and inclinations may not themselves be morally good or bad, but we are morally responsible for the manner in which we react to them (398). Whenever we do act immorally, it is only because we have yielded to their lure. When they compete with moral requirements, they constitute what Kant called

131

"subjective limitations and obstacles" to our striving for good moral character (397, 413). Kant did not think it necessarily better that we sometimes happen to want what is morally obligatory, for then it is easy for us to waver between acting on moral motives and acting on nonmoral motives (411). Moreover, "to the extent that something empirical is added to [moral motives], just this much is subtracted from their genuine influence and from the unqualified worth of actions" (411). Indeed, since inclinations tend to gain strength the more we indulge them, the more we rely on them, the more we also risk acting on them when it is immoral to do so (394).

Consequently, in the *Foundations,* Kant emphasized how our desires and inclinations can be "subjective hindrances to" and "a powerful counterweight to" the moral law (397, 405).[2] They tempt us to "argue against the stern laws of duty and their validity, or at least to place their purity and strictness in doubt and, where possible, to make them more accordant with our wishes and inclinations" (405). In that book, he took a strict stance: We must not use the desire for pleasure to motivate ourselves to obey the moral law, for that would destroy the moral worth of our actions.

It is important to add immediately that this is only part of Kant's doctrine concerning desires. For example, as we shall see at the end of this chapter, we have a great deal of leeway in deciding how to fulfill our positive moral duties, and then for the most part our judgments *must* be made on the basis of our desires and preferences. In those cases, we do not depend on our desires to help motivate us to obey the Categorical Imperative. That is, we are not using desires to "prop up" our will to do what is right. Rather, because the Categorical Imperative offers us no guidance beyond very general directions, we have no alternative save to make many of our particular decisions on the basis of our personal feelings and preferences. This need not weaken our commitment to the moral law, if we still dutifully avoid doing what we ought not to do.

THE "RADICAL EVIL" IN HUMAN NATURE

What led Kant to take such a harsh view of human emotions in the *Foundations* was the fact that, when he thought about the comparative strengths of reason and of desire and about the frequency of moral failures, he concluded that we do not just experience "neutral" choices between the moral law and our desires. Instead, we often find ourselves feeling reluctant to acknowledge the requirements of the moral law within us, so that we have to make a positive *effort* to act dutifully. By contrast, we seem naturally inclined to act immorally when that promises pleasure or seems to promote self-interest. In support of his view, Kant pointed out how the historical record shows the continual proclivity of the human race to commit the most terrible crimes imaginable.

In one of his later books, *Religion within the Limits of Reason Alone*, Kant pushed his analysis of the human moral predicament further than he did in the *Foundations*. There he wrote that we find ourselves in an "ethical state of nature"; we all have a radical, innate, and irradicable tendency to resist the moral law. In his analysis, we all tend to regard ourselves as living in an amoral Hobbesian world of unrelenting hostility toward and competition with others, whom we regard as either instruments or obstacles in our quest to satisfy our desires for possessions and power.

Kant held that children become moral beings only with the emergence of reason, which enables the moral law to appear in their self-awareness, inexorably commanding their obedience. Consequently, each of us has what he called an innate "predisposition" toward having a morally good character consisting of an irradicable recognition that we are obligated to respect and obey the moral law. In that sense, he concluded, everyone can be considered originally morally good by nature. And that, he also wrote, is why human moral agents cannot be totally depraved and irrevocably evil, unable to do anything morally good, as portrayed in the traditional doctrine of Original Sin.

How then can we account for the predisposition to evil? If our moral character depends only on our own free decisions, it must be a tendency for which each of us is responsible. We should not try to blame it on some part of our nature (such as our inclinations) or on the decisions or influence of some other person or persons (such as a biblical Adam or one's parents). Kant was therefore led to believe that we are so attracted to pleasure and repelled by pain that we all initially choose to satisfy our desires rather than obey the moral law. The consequence is that the effort to adopt a morally virtuous disposition always begins with a will *already* resisting the demands of morality and requiring what Kant called a moral revolution to reject its initial "fall." That, he thought, is the kernel of truth in the doctrine of Original Sin.

Kant concluded that the Stoics (and most other philosophers as well) had underestimated the strength of this opposition to the moral law. They had thought that moral development begins with a simple need to curb and train the undisciplined desires of the child. On the contrary, he wrote in his *Religion within the Limits of Reason Alone,* "We cannot start from an innocence natural to us but must begin with the assumption of a wickedness of the will in adopting its maxims contrary to the original [good] moral predisposition." The internal moral conflict everyone experiences, therefore, is a struggle between an innate predisposition to good and a radical acquired tendency toward evil that never seems to be eradicated.

In Chapter 5 we saw that Kant believed that the only hope for widespread success in the universal struggle against radical evil lies with the establishment and spread of an ethical society, a universal religion, as the third formula commands.

THE ULTIMATE COMMITMENT

Out of this internal moral conflict comes either virtue or vice, for either our reason or our desires will dominate our decisions (400). The continuing press of individual moral decisions eventually forces us to commit ourselves to a single, ultimate, overriding practical principle, *either* to conform to the Law of Autonomy and subordinate everything else to it *or* to subordinate it to the principle of self-love. Since no one can avoid making an ultimate choice of moral character, Kant held that no one can have a morally indifferent character. Unless reason holds the reins of government in its own hands, he warned, our feelings and inclinations will certainly assume mastery over us. Either we deliberately and with some effort adopt the motive of duty, or we inevitably will end up acting only on maxims of self-love, that is, only on prudential motives.

The adoption of a supreme practical principle is a unique exercise of our freedom in the sense that it does not presuppose any more ultimate ground, such as the adoption of some end or other; instead, it is itself the ultimate norm for whatever ends we do adopt. Likewise, it is not influenced by any incentives but instead is decisive in determining which incentives will prevail. Because it is an utterly free commitment, we cannot hope to understand how anyone goes about adopting such a disposition (460, 462).

Kant was well aware that even the best of us would have lapses of moral weakness, and he also knew it would be easy to develop what he called an "impure will," in which our moral motivation is partly sustained by prudential interests. But both such failings, he wrote, indicate a lack of virtue rather than that a person is morally evil. The real opponent and opposite of virtue is vice, which consists in embracing the principle of self-love as one's basic principle, adopting the intention or disposition to transgress the moral law whenever it conflicts with the possibility of pleasures one wants.

Vice does not consist in acting on individual inclinations, as happens when there is moral weakness, but in acting on a settled immoral disposition. The evil person has calmly and deliberately adopted the immoral policy always to satisfy his or her inclinations. Because even the morally worst persons still possess moral reason, vice cannot cause invincible ignorance that might excuse them from moral responsibility for the evil they do. For the same reason, Kant also held that human beings can never develop a diabolical, that is, a *totally* evil, character; that would require the complete rejection of the moral law *because* it is the moral law and the deliberate and defiant choice of the evil principle just because it is evil. Nonetheless, Kant did think that moral vice may be incurable, not because a person loses free choice but because, as Aristotle had said, "the patient does not want to be cured."[3]

A consistent pattern of morally legal or illegal actions, especially over the course of a person's whole life, gives us some grounds to infer the corresponding ultimate internal maxim. But we may still err when making such judgments. We can judge actions as morally legal or not, but we cannot be certain about the quality of the moral character in which they originate, for character always depends on maxims that we cannot see (407). It is possible, for example, for an individual habitually to perform legally correct actions only because they happen to fit that person's conception of happiness, but we cannot know if or when this happens. In fact, we can never be certain about the quality of our own character, and for that reason we need constantly to avow anew the ultimate maxim of good character, while we hope we are only reaffirming a commitment already made.

MORAL INTEREST

When surveying Kant's general account of intelligent agency in the preceding chapter, we saw that he was convinced that, because we have a sensuous nature, we will not act unless we first have desires or aversions to give us an *incentive* for acting. Prudential actions can always be explained by citing the satisfaction of some desire or other that gave us an interest in acting. Since dutifulness may require us to set aside considerations of our own happiness and welfare, it makes sense to ask what can possibly serve as an incentive to *interest* us in acting dutifully. Even when we know what our duty is and that it is our duty, we can still reasonably ask why we should *care* about doing our duty.

In the case of a purely rational being, there would be no distance between the cognitive and the conative functions of reason, for it is the nature of such a being always and necessarily to act on the Law of Autonomy (414, 449). However, that is not the case with imperfectly rational agents like us; we can refuse to do what we know morality requires. That is why Kant held that our moral reason must be able to generate specifically *moral sentiments* that can function as moral incentives, so powerful that they can overpower every incentive that happiness might offer in opposition (461).

Kant has frequently been read as claiming that moral action requires us to act in the complete absence of desires of any kind. It is true that he did insist that acting only on the desire for pleasure is just what makes our actions merely heteronomous; even when actions motivated by such desires are morally unobjectionable, they still have no moral worth (398, 444). However, he also held that there *must* be a feeling side to *human* morality (432, 460). Other moral agents (like God) may not need moral incentives, but for sensuous beings like ourselves, not only *can* moral reason impact on that part of us which it judges and, when necessary, frustrates, but it *must* do so (413n). This claim is confirmed by the emotions we in fact do feel when we are confronted by duty, when we act dutifully, and when we do not.

MORAL SENTIMENTS

Moral sentiments are like nonmoral emotions in the sense that they are felt somatically or, in Kant's terminology, pathologically. Since Kant classified all feelings under the titles of pleasure and pain, moral sentiments must also involve pleasure or pain or a combination of the two. Moreover, like nonmoral emotions, they are also subjective in the sense that they are necessary for subjects like us who need sensuous moral incentives to feel morally obligated.[4] If moral sentiments were *completely* like all other desires, however, it would be true that morality is nothing but prudence.

Thus, Kant argued that moral sentiments differ from other, what he called *"merely* pathological," feelings and desires in two critical ways. First, they do not have their origin in causes outside our own reason so that we only passively feel them (401n, 403). Rather, they are self-produced, for they are the subjective effect of our *prior* recognition of the absolute binding force of the moral law. Second, because that awareness causes these feelings, acting morally does not mean we are acting *out of* desire; it is still the moral law that is the ultimate motive for our interest in acting morally (416, 449, 460). When we experience *merely* pathological desires, we take something to be good just because we desire it, but when we experience moral desires, we desire something because we first have determined that it is good on the basis of a prior moral judgment (413n, 459n). To put the same point in a somewhat different way, morality does not obligate us because we first find ourselves interested in it; rather, we find we are interested in the moral law because we first recognize that we are obligated by it (449, 460–1).

We do not have a duty to have moral sentiments, Kant held, since we already have them and irresistibly so by virtue of our consciousness of the moral law within us. Even "the most hardened scoundrel" cannot totally avoid feeling them (454–5). But because we can be more or less sensitive to such feelings and so also to the moral law, it *is* our duty to cultivate and strengthen them.

Finally, the effect of our acting out of specifically moral interest – acting as duty requires – will not appear to an observer to be different from our engaging in the same behavior for prudential reasons. From the point of view of psychology, moral respect, for example, must be regarded as an emotion like all other emotions, caused by some prior cause or causes such as parental training. Nonetheless, from the practical point of view, moral sentiments do not function as causal explanations; and they are not themselves explicable in naturalistic, that is, in deterministic and nonmoral, terms (460). Rather, they are the somatic effect only of our moral reason impacting on us as human agents with a moral life that is permeated by emotions.

RESPECT AND OTHER MORAL SENTIMENTS

The *only* specifically moral incentive that can motivate us to act dutifully, Kant wrote, is the reverence or respect we unavoidably feel for the moral law (440). In fact, it is because we all inevitably experience respect for the moral law that, as we have just seen, Kant held that we have a predisposition to be morally good. As an emotion, respect resembles fear of (aversion to) pain in that we recognize that the moral law may rightfully demand the denial of self-love; it also is something like love (attraction) in the sense that we recognize that that law originates in our own reason and is something we impose upon ourselves (401n). Moreover, it is an incentive of such strength that it enables us, when necessary, to offset the influence of all our inclinations (400,

401n, 446). For agents like us humans, then, respect for the moral law is the subjectively necessary side of our consciousness of duty.

So important a role in our moral life does respect have that Kant included respect in his third "proposition" about the human good will in the *Foundations*, defining "duty" as "the necessity to act from respect for [the moral] law" (400). In his defense of human moral agency in the third section of that work, he reintroduced the topic of moral interest to block any attempt to try to explain human moral agency as caused by merely pathological desires and inclinations (459–61).

Since the moral law is the law of our own reason, the virtuous person is one who acts out of self-respect, and self-respect is the subjectively necessary ground for our fulfilling *all* our duties. Likewise, "love for one's neighbor" expresses the same moral esteem in which, according to the universal requirement of the Categorical Imperative, we must hold all other persons. The ultimate subjective moral appeal in human moral life, then, is to self-respect and to an equal respect for all other persons. As we have seen, each of us has dignity that prevents us from ever legitimately regarding ourselves or others as only conditionally valuable, that is, valuable only to the extent of being the object of someone's inclinations.

In his other writings Kant mentioned additional moral feelings. They include humility, that is, an awareness of our propensity to pursue pleasure even when doing so is immoral; pain when the moral law frustrates our inclinations; moral contentment or satisfaction, that is, a feeling of greater moral worth, when we do our duty (396, 454–5, 460);[5] guilt and remorse when we disobey the moral law; empathy with the joys and sorrows of others as fellow moral beings; and hope, the confidence that if we do what we ought, we eventually will have the happiness we deserve.

As important as moral sentiments are, they cannot serve as

the basis for our moral judgments. They are still only subjective feelings, not objective judgments about what we should and should not do (460).

The moral law "disregards, as it were, and holds in contempt" all the claims of our inclinations (405).[6] Moreover, commanding someone to do something gladly is self-contradictory, Kant wrote, because commands are necessary only within a context of at least potential reluctance and opposition (412–14). Understandably, many of his readers have been repelled by his apparently gray and cheerless delineation of human moral life.

Kant wryly noted that we are not volunteers in the moral world; instead, we find ourselves conscripted into the discipline of duty. Although it is typical of our fallen nature to react to the demands of morality with reluctance, he also insisted that what one does unwillingly, morosely, or cheerlessly, one does poorly. Consequently, he saw our moral life through a pair of spectacles ground to fit the eyes of an eighteenth century, enlightened, Christian, Stoic moral teacher. He did not believe our moral life could be reduced to a life of pleasure, but he also did not believe that a truly virtuous life should be dreary and bleak.

Kant's ideal moral personality turns out to be very much like the ancient Stoic ideal of the person who has developed emotional self-constraint and who finds an inner tranquillity in the performance of duty. Such a serene and joyous frame of mind, he thought, is the best evidence that a person really is committed to a conscientious observance of the moral law. Since we should promote the happiness of others insofar as we can, he also wrote that a person of good moral character should not be a bore but should give pleasure to his or her friends; and he spent a good deal of time discussing ways in which a good person might practice sociability.

It is within the context of the spirit of virtuous morality that we can best approach Kant's discussion of types of "moral fanaticism."

Given his analysis of human nature, he thought it a mistake to think we can become so confirmed in goodness that we no longer experience morality as our duty but will act rightly simply because it is the beautiful and noble thing to do. Likewise, if we try to develop and maintain an intense moral enthusiasm, we will find it cannot last and will leave only a feeling of flat depression in its wake, showing that enthusiasm is not a moral emotion at all. This is the place for the Stoic ideal of moderation: genuine virtue requires a calm and firm commitment to act as one should.

Another form of fanaticism, Kant thought, consists in believing, out of superstitious fear of a vengeful God, that in place of genuine repentance for our moral failings, we must atone for them by rituals and penances. In a related way, he also held that it is fanaticism about dutifulness itself to *overly* discipline our inclinations by trying to renounce all enjoyment of life. As we have already seen, for the sake of our own virtue, we may even have an indirect duty to promote our own happiness, for too many unfulfilled wants create their own temptations to transgress our duties.

Finally, it also is a type of moral fanaticism, Kant held, to insist that morally trivial differences, as, for example, between meat and fish or between beer and wine, have serious moral importance. Finding duties everywhere – what he somewhat sarcastically called "fantastic virtue" – turns the sovereignty of moral claims into a tyranny.

MIXED MOTIVATION

Kant believed that the motive of dutifulness is most evident when it costs us happiness by requiring us to act directly contrary to our desires and aversions (397, 415, 431). When people reading Kant for the first time measure themselves against his theory of moral motivation, they invariably find that many, perhaps most, of their actions that have conformed to duty also have presented the means to some end or other that they in fact also desired. They therefore conclude that they often have acted from "mixed motivation," that is, both from the motive of duty and from prudential motives. What, according to Kant, is the moral value of acting from mixed motives? This is a complicated topic, and it is not easy to get a clear perspective on what he thought.

In the *Foundations,* Kant emphasized that if an action is to have moral value for us, we need to recognize the specifically moral value in that action and then act on that recognition. Accordingly, acting on the basis only of a desire for pleasure has no moral worth, and desires need to be regarded as rivals to morality. When we act from mixed motivation, therefore, we are virtuous *only* insofar as we do what we ought because we are motivated to do so by the moral law. "We cannot too much or too often," Kant wrote, warn against relying on contingent, empirical inducements *to help motivate* us to act rightly (426). Deliberately introducing prudential considerations as motives makes our will morally "impure," and cultivating an impure will, even when done with good intent, is but one step away from giving nonmoral incentives precedence over the moral motive of duty (411).

This is far from the whole story, however. In the *Foundations,* Kant's analysis of moral motivation is limited to considering only individual decisions, apart from how their moral quality might be affected by an agent's character. It was also from this point of view that he claimed that actions have no moral value when they are performed by people with so sympathetic a temper that they enjoy making others happy (398). Probably nothing else he wrote has been criticized more frequently or fervently than this view. Most readers believe Kant was wrong to deny such actions *all* moral worth.

SYMPATHY AND MORAL WORTH

As it turns out, within the context of Kant's *entire* moral theory, the criticism is a valid enunciation of ordinary moral reasoning. The best way to show this is to point out that in the *Foundations* Kant in effect held that, taken in abstraction from other considerations, there are morally indifferent actions, that is, actions not contrary to the moral law but still without moral worth. But is it possible, within the total Kantian theory, for a *person* to act in a completely morally indifferent manner? Kant could address this question only after he had developed his doctrine of character in his *Religion within the Limits of Reason Alone,* published eight years after the *Foundations.* There he held that the only morally indifferent agents are those that are nonrational and the only morally indifferent actions are those determined by natural causal laws. By contrast, moral agents *cannot* have a morally indifferent character; they *necessarily* have either a good or an evil ultimate disposition.

So pervasive is character in our moral life, Kant argued, that all the expressions of a morally good will have some moral worth, even if, because of invincible ignorance, they involve acting on wrong maxims. Likewise, none of the choices arising out of a morally evil will can be morally worthy, even when, taken abstractly, the behavior at least is not morally forbidden.

As we have seen, we have a positive duty to contribute to the welfare and happiness of others, but in the absence of other moral obligations, the Categorical Imperative does not offer us precise guidance about how to do so. So the only rational criteria available to us in this part of our moral life are mainly prudential in nature. The prudential judgments we make in order to fulfill our positive duties, then, are an extension of our moral judgment. As we have seen, Kant held that good judgment is an ability we need to develop.

What Kant neglected to say in the *Foundations* is that the moral law now reminds us that our prudential judgments should be made thoughtfully and well so that we live up to the worth we have as moral persons. For example, although the moral law does not tell us precisely whom to care about or just how to do so, we still need to exercise good judgment about whom we choose as our friends; we should look for people who will sustain and support the quality of our life, including its moral quality. With that demur in mind, we clearly may develop special affections and pay special attention to some people rather than others; we also are free to devote ourselves to those causes about which we particularly care; and we are well advised to choose occupations we are likely to enjoy and do well. Positive duties also do not demand that we become moral drudges; they give us recess time, so to speak, so that we can devote ourselves to morally permissible activities we simply enjoy. There are no hard and fast rules to determine just how to weigh such judgments. In all such cases, however, insofar as a person's actions are chosen within a prior commitment to the moral law, they *are* the actions of a morally good person.

If, therefore, some of us naturally have "so sympathetic a temper that, without any motive of vanity or selfishness, [we] find an inner satisfaction in spreading joy and rejoice in the contentment of others which [we] have made possible," our actions clearly *can* and *do* have "true moral worth" (398), as long as we continue to be faithful to the moral law. In all such cases we do not – indeed cannot – leave our moral characters behind, and we therefore cannot act in an amoral fashion; if we are good people, we are committed to the moral law as our supreme ultimate disposition.

To review quickly, morality enters into these kinds of choices in two ways. The first is as a limiting condition. In the case of sympathetic actions, the moral law would constrain us from acting compassionately toward others, for example, if doing so would be detrimental to their autonomy and self-respect. (In this way morality supports only constructive relations between persons.) The fact that our character permeates our life through and through means that the moral law also plays a second role, approving and supporting our prudential choices when we make them wisely. The selection of a vocation that helps others, for example, can hardly be merely a morally indifferent matter but involves a commitment to both a natural and a moral good. (In this way our life in this world can anticipate our total final good, which is a complex of both such goods.)

The enduring presence and influence of good moral character ensure that our emotions, even those that initially were only inherited temperamental qualities, can serve to *complement*, rather than compete with, morality, leading our judgments in ways that are morally legitimate. In the *Foundations*, Kant had little to say about these more specific choices, for what a person might say about contingent and particular matters tends to have only limited value to others; what may contribute, for example, to the fulfillment of one person may only promote dependency and sloth in another. However, in the preface to the *Foundations*, he did note that exploring the more specific applications of our moral life requires "practical anthropology" (388). When we read the notes we have from his anthropology class (his favorite course, we are told), we may be struck by how much of what one might say in these matters is influenced by one's culture. For that reason, Kant's *Anthropology* is only infrequently discussed; it may be the least influential part of his moral writings.

When fulfilling our positive duties, clearly we are in fact acting from mixed motives, but not in the sense that Kant condemned in the *Foundations*. We are not using desires to buttress our moral disposition, nor are we constructing a private morality of the sort Kant condemned, in which desires compete with and replace genuine moral motivation. Rather, in the case of positive duties, we act from desires because we *need* to do so *in order* to obey the moral law. (Our actions can, of course, still be interpreted as evidences only of our empirical character, for, as Kant repeatedly pointed out, the ultimate disposition underlying our actions and uniting them as expressions of moral character is not open to plain view.)

It is no wonder, then, that we think we have often acted from mixed motives; our problem is to try to be as sure as possible that we have acted from mixed motives in a morally acceptable sense. In this matter, once again, Kant would have insisted, first, that we cannot have complete certainty and, second, that the fact we must rely so often and so heavily on our desires unfortunately can contribute to that very rivalry with which he was preoccupied in the *Foundations*.

NOTES

1. Kant argued that ordinary people do not have a great deal of difficulty recognizing the radical difference between moral and prudential incentives (404) and, therefore, in their self-awareness, can distinguish between conflicts involving only pathological desires and conflicts between such desires and duty.
2. For this reason Kant made the otherwise startling claim that "the universal wish of every rational being must be indeed to free himself completely from" all desires (428; see 454). We act immorally only because we have desires; we have desires only because we have needs; and it would be better not to have any needs at all.
3. Kant's analysis of moral virtue as strength forced him to conclude that moral evil is a lack of power, especially rational strength. Individuals like Stalin and Hitler suggest, to the contrary, that there can be evil people whose lives evidence unusual rational, yet immoral, strength. Evil remains ultimately incomprehensible.
4. Kant used the term "subjective" in two very different senses. In one sense, "subjective" refers to the subject or human agent (or conditions in that agent) and contrasts with what is "given" from

outside the agent in some sense or other, such as objects given in experience. In the second sense, "subjective" refers to what is arbitrary and thus peculiar to individual agents, in contrast to what is objective and holds necessarily and universally for all rational agents or at least for all human agents. Moral emotions are subjective in the first sense, for they reside in the human moral agent and, because they do, are the subjective foundation of human morality. They are also subjective in the second sense, because their strength can vary from person to person. But because they are generated by the objective moral law, they are not *completely* subjective in the second sense, as are our likes and dislikes.

5. Moral contentment can only follow from our consciousness of having acted dutifully, and we can act dutifully only if we *set aside* all consideration of how acting dutifully may affect us personally. To argue, then, that our motive for acting virtuously is anticipation of the contentment we feel after having acted dutifully is to make an incoherent claim, involving an internal contradiction. As Kant pointed out, if we could be moved to do our duty only in order to feel good afterward, we could never act dutifully and therefore never experience moral contentment!

6. If they are not understood to be only partial statements of Kant's beliefs, statements such as this can easily give rise to the common misinterpretation that Kant had no regard at all for human welfare and happiness. Those who read mainly the *Foundations* can end up with a very skewed understanding of Kant's views on moral emotions.

9

LIVING UNDER THE MORAL LAW

W E have already encountered many of our moral duties
when examining Kant's explication of the Categorical
Imperative in the *Foundations;* others he discussed elsewhere,
particularly in his *Metaphysics of Morals.* In this chapter, we again
look at all those that Kant discussed, but in a more organized
way. This inventory will not bring anything surprising to light,
since he aimed only to reflect what he called "common moral
knowledge." We would not expect every detail of a moral code
that is almost two hundred years old to endure without any
need for changes, but the very fact that so many of his judgments have survived largely intact is strong presumptive evidence of their fundamental rightness.

We have seen that, according to Kant, we have various kinds
of duties. Some are negative; others, positive. Some we have
because we are moral agents affected by desires and, therefore,
are only contingently obedient to the moral law, and others
we have only because we are finite moral–physical beings. We
will organize all these duties by asking three questions:

1. What kind of political system should we have?
2. What kind of person should each of us aim to become?
3. What should our personal associations be like?

These questions will help us review our different duties in the
same order as in the preceding chapters, beginning with those
requirements for living together in a civil community. Following this arrangement should also give us a reasonably coherent
view of human life, for all three moral areas share the same

foundational practical standard, expressed either as the Principle of Justice or in the various formulas of the Categorical Imperative.

We have good reason to review that standard now before becoming more specific, since dividing our moral life into areas can lead to the same mistake that has sometimes been occasioned by Kant's separate discussions of our various duties in the *Foundations*. According to that misinterpretation, Kant thought that human moral life consists only of various discrete choices that lack any common thread of continuity uniting them into a single life. It is true that the clarity to which moral theorizing aspires does require us to examine various parts of our moral life individually and sequentially. But this should not overshadow what Kant described as the "absolute unity" of that life based on an overriding commitment to the Law of Autonomy. This commitment, rightly made, should ensure that whatever our specific concerns and engagements, our moral life should have an underlying seamlessness, a unity, an integrity of the self grounded in our character. We therefore need to keep in mind that each of the areas and each of the duties of human moral life discussed in the following pages constitutes but part of a single moral commitment that should permeate every area of our lives.

THE FOUNDATION OF MORALITY

The first formula, an enriched variation of the political Principle of Justice, is that version of the Categorical Imperative that we may be most apt to use in public life, because so many of our moral problems there concern justice and fairness:

> Never act except in such a way that you can also will that your maxims should become universal laws. (Adapted from 402)

150

This principle is the foundation for political self-determination in contrast to tyranny. As a negative norm of external freedom, it also constrains those tendencies we have to violate the person, the autonomy, and/or the property of others.

This formula also is helpful in clarifying the nature of morality in our personal lives, for it is the foundation for ethical self-determination in contrast to a life dominated by some external authority. It also requires the subordination of self-love to the requirements of morality, so that no interest we may have can lie beyond the reach of its judgment.

When we turn to considerations of benevolence, happiness, and personal virtue, all positive obligations, it is the second formula that may most often seem the more appropriate norm:

> Act so that you treat humanity, whether in your own person or in that of another, always as an end and never as a means only. (429)

This formula, however, only echoes what the first formula also insists on: that we recognize the worth of all rational beings, others as well as ourselves. What is mandated is an attitude and a commitment underlying everything else in our practical lives: respect for our own worth as free, rational persons capable of what nothing else in creation can do, namely, living our lives on the basis of our own decisions and laws of our own making. We are also to respect others, for they too share the same freedom, rationality, and legislative capacity.

WHAT KIND OF POLITICAL SYSTEM SHOULD WE HAVE?

Throughout our lives, we depend on a civil society to help us achieve our goals and protect our interests and our life and property, thereby ensuring an environment within which we have the freedom to develop and exercise our abilities and pursue both happiness and virtue. As a law of reciprocity, the moral law insists that we not isolate ourselves from the society within which we live. We have a duty, insofar as we can, to support and contribute to the political community to which we belong and to which we are so deeply indebted.

Kant believed that the most fundamental internal problem for any state is the fact that people remain in what he called an "ethical state of nature." That is, there is a widespread tendency for people to be concerned only with satisfying their own desires and, as a consequence, to treat each other in an insensitive and hostile fashion. No state, therefore, can allow its citizens to act just on their desires; to do so would be to guarantee the disintegration of the structure of society. The fundamental laws of a state need to be mainly negative, constraining people from misusing others or interfering with others' lawful pursuit of their interests. Since the observance of civil law cannot rest on any confidence that the citizens are all morally conscientious people, civil order must be enforced by coercion and by the threat of sanctions.

Kant held that only a state that is a republic at least in spirit will institutionalize those reciprocal relations that morally should hold between free and rational people. Such a state has laws that the citizens themselves could have enacted even if they in fact do not have the legal right to be self-legislative. The requirement that the state should respect all the citizens means that its legal structure needs a moral ground, namely, the Universal Principle of Justice. We saw that Kant argued that the rightness of this principle is self-evident, for its denial results in a formula for chaos. It requires two things: that laws hold universally and impersonally, thereby avoiding partiality toward special interest; and that laws be such that every person could agree to their enactment after setting aside considerations of self-interest.

The very formality of the Principle of Justice means that it cannot be applied directly to our individual decisions. But we do need it to generate intermediate-level, substantive moral principles that will limit each person's pursuit of his or her own desires and interests in a lawful fashion by the equal entitlement of others to the pursuit of their interests. We saw in Chapter 1 that principles like these create the legal framework for the public moral world and that like the Principle of Justice itself, their correctness can be seen by reason alone; that is, their denial will result in practical contradictions of one sort or another.

As Kant also pointed out, these intermediate-level laws are so general, of the kind that might be included in a Bill of Duties (for Kant, more fundamental than a Bill of Rights), that they need to be supplemented by more specific, "positive" laws. These must not conflict with the higher-level laws, but, for example, like a code of taxation mandating that those with larger incomes should bear a greater share of the tax burden, they may need to recognize differences between various groups of citizens. Since such laws must still reflect the general requirement of fairness, their enactment and enforcement must be done in an impersonal manner that ignores exactly which specific individuals fall under them.

Even the legislation of positive laws does not determine all our particular civic duties. As we saw in Chapter 2, when there are no additional rules to span the distance between the laws of society and our individual judgments, the latter constitute a further exercise of our ability and our need to reason practically. Our obligations to the state are two-dimensional: to act as lawgivers, legislating, at least through a representative government, laws that conform to the Principle of Justice; and as citizens, to obey those same laws. Although the state cannot legislate submission to its laws from the motive of duty, our own obedience to legitimate civil authority is, in fact, an ethical obligation.

In general terms, simply taking the normal duties of citizenship seriously means respecting that system of laws that rests on and promotes respect for everyone, oneself included. That clearly means living in a law-abiding fashion and allowing and encouraging others to do so as well. Given his conviction that the primary need for laws arises out of our tendency to pursue our own aims at the expense of others, Kant stressed those negative laws curtailing behaviors that undercut the possibility of our living together in a just society. We may not treat others unjustly, in ways to which they cannot rationally assent, by violating their external rights.

Finally, we may not be completely indifferent to the happiness and well-being of our fellow citizens. We should practice universal benevolence by willing the happiness of all others, and insofar as we can, we should help provide the basic needs of those unable to provide for themselves.

WHAT KIND OF PERSON SHOULD I AIM TO BECOME?

According to Kant, the most important single moral fact about us is that we possess autonomy; we have the ability to make our own decisions and to live by them rather than being totally subject to determination by the laws of natural causality like other kinds of agents in the world. Our most fundamental duty, therefore, is to exercise our autonomy and at least strive to achieve a perfectly moral character: doing our duty, whatever it might be, and doing it from the specifically moral motive that it is our duty. We need to make a commitment to the moral law as the ultimate source of value in our lives, for the worth of everything else we do depends on that commitment. The overriding question should be, What kind of persons are we making of ourselves? And the answer we should be able to give is that we are doing everything we can to cultivate self-respect. More than anything else, that will motivate us to become the sort of person we should be and to live the sort of life we should live.

The second most fundamental moral fact about us, Kant

thought, is our experience of internal moral conflict. Because we so frequently must concern ourselves with our own needs and make decisions about our welfare based on the law of prudence, we are constantly tempted to adopt the law of self-love as our ultimate practical principle. We need to keep our priorities straight and recognize that our pursuit of happiness is always subject to limitation by the moral law.

In our personal life we are not exempt from any of the negative obligations of justice that constrain us in our public life. But in our private life we are also subject to constant temptations to neglect or diminish or deny our sense of our own worth, whether by attitudes such as miserly avarice or servility or by actions like lying in which we regard ourselves as being valuable only insofar as we serve some use by satisfying our own or someone else's desires. Most of us must also struggle against the vice of laziness or sloth, which tempts us to neglect either our mental or our physical well-being, both of which can promote our ability to flourish as moral agents. Kant added that we also may not to do anything that might specifically contribute to or cause the destruction of ourselves physically, whether by excessive food or drink or drugs, by self-mutilation, or by suicide.

In the *Foundations* Kant's third example emphasized our positive duty to strive for nonmoral perfection in the sense of cultivating our talents. He complained that parents see to it that their children learn all sorts of things that might be useful later on but neglect to discuss "the *worth* of the things which [the children] may make their ends" (415). As a champion of the Enlightenment, he argued that taking the second formula of the Categorical Imperative seriously should motivate us to develop those natural gifts we have and to commit ourselves to those kinds of activities that will enhance and deepen our sense of self-respect by contributing to worthwhile goals. This includes the cultivation of our mental gifts as well as caring for our psychological and physical health. (We have seen that natural goods become also morally obligatory ends for us when they are necessary or helpful for our living dutifully.)

The possibilities open to us depend on so many contingencies – on what talents we do or do not have and on what opportunities do or do not come our way – that little more specific can be proposed by a moral theory, in advance of our considering particular cases. Kant was only too well aware of how little opportunity the Prussian peasants had to develop their talents, and he did not want to propose a theory that would imply they were due less respect because of the limitations imposed on them by their country's political system. But he still thought that it is morally wrong for us *deliberately* to neglect those traits that can maintain and strengthen our ability to act morally. As is the case with other positive duties, we have a good deal of moral latitude about which to develop and how far to do so.

Finally, we have an indirect duty to tend to our own happiness and well-being when that is necessary or helpful to living a morally good life. But it is unnecessarily moralistic to think of this only in terms of being a duty. Within the parameters of the moral law, our sense of self-worth should motivate us not only to care about and pursue our own morally permissible welfare and happiness but also to promote those of others.

WHAT SHOULD OUR PERSONAL ASSOCIATIONS BE LIKE?

We humans are not by nature radical individuals; our sense of identity and of personal worth cannot be developed or lived completely apart from our relationships of mutual dependence with others. We need to join with others in voluntary relationships of varying closeness and formality. The fact that such associations can fulfill our needs and enhance the quality of our lives implies that we may have a moral obligation to enter into *some* such attachments. Other things being equal, however, our choices (e.g., to join this group rather than that one or to pursue a friendship with this individual rather than that one) clearly are morally permissible decisions to be made on the basis of prudential considerations.

Once we are in a relationship, however, the negative norms of public morality continue to set limits on the roles we assume, as well as on our actions and attitudes. (To put Kant's doctrine in current terms, public morality may condemn and intervene in cases of child abuse and spouse abuse.) Kant was particularly sensitive to the ways in which the government and the aristocracy treated the peasants, thereby violating their right to respect. To respect all others as we should, he wrote, we may not regard or treat them merely as the means to our own ends, without regard for their intrinsic worth, as happens in the case of lies and lying promises. He also specifically mentioned mean attitudes evincing envy, malice, ingratitude, pride, or vengefulness; and he condemned behaviors that degrade others, such as calumny, slander, ridicule, arrogance, and contempt. We also may not make it more difficult for others to pursue their own moral obligations, although what this duty entails varies with the people involved and the circumstances.

Kant limited his remarks about sexual morality to negative duties. He did not discuss the topic at all in the *Foundations*, but in his other writings he defended a view shared by almost everyone until relatively recently: that sexual activity is tied irrevocably to procreation. He argued that it is immoral to frustrate that purpose deliberately. (Because technology has enabled us to sever the tie between sexual activity and procreation, this has become a minority view today, and deep differences about the *point* of various kinds of sexual activity are reflected in correspondingly deep differences over their morality.) One Kantian claim that seems to have survived intact is his judgment that any sexual activity is immoral that denigrates another person by using that person merely as an object for the sake of pleasure, as in impersonal sex.

What can be said in a positive way about our personal affiliations depends greatly on the type of affiliation. Our relations with others can take many different forms – from business associations, to memberships in groups sharing a common interest, to casual friendships, to intimate associations such as marriage. Such affiliations are typically based on commonalities, but as Aristotle pointed out, they can be motivated differently – by utility, pleasure, or caring for others for their own sake.

Once beyond the negative norms, we are in the arena of prudential judgments, with counsels that hold, when they do, only for the most part. So much depends on the particular circumstances of one's situation. Judgments of moral relevance in a relationship, for example, may depend on what happens to be important to the other person or persons, and that, of course, will vary from person to person. Standards of conduct will also vary from one kind of association to another, and the further we move from generalities to more specific descriptions of how we should conduct such relationships, the less important place there seems to be for rules, except for their offering very general negative boundaries. The more fluid a relationship, the more we have to rely on what Kant called judgment and what Aristotle referred to as practical perceptiveness.

Clearly, we should contribute to the lives of others insofar as that is appropriate and possible. As is the case with our other positive duties, we have a good deal of latitude about exactly how to do this. Beyond that, perhaps the most important observation to make is that personal relations deepen and narrow the nature of reciprocity in significant positive ways: Whereas the essence of public morality is impartiality, the essence of personal relations is *partiality*. (In that sense, within the negative parameters already mentioned, personal standards of conduct can be quite different from public standards.) In fact, Kant held that morality typically *requires* special loyalties. The closer a relationship becomes, the more we should think from the standpoint of others in the relationship, the more we should empathetically identify with their projects and needs, and the more we should care about and support the fulfillment of their concerns and commitments (what Kant called their "ends"). Our respect for the intrinsic value of others is shown by sensitivity to what is important to them. There are still limits, of course; we should not, for example, violate the autonomy of others by assuming responsibility for their happiness or by imposing on others our own ideas about what should make them happy.

In his *Metaphysics of Morals* Kant portrayed friendship as a microcosm of human moral life. As "the union of two persons through equal and mutual love and respect," friendship spans and embodies the tensions between our emotional and moral interests. Emotional love, he wrote, tends to draw people closer together, thereby threatening their respect for one another, whereas moral respect limits intimacy by requiring us not to become "too familiar" with one another.

10

THE DEFENSE OF MORALITY
(*FOUNDATIONS* 3)

IN the first two sections of the *Foundations,* Kant analyzed what it must mean to say that human beings are moral agents. His analysis yielded this claim: if our common belief is correct, we are moral agents to whom the Law of Autonomy must appear as a categorical imperative (414, 432). What the analysis of concepts by itself could not show is that we really are moral agents (425, 445). But Kant remarked that just formulating the ultimate moral law "more precisely than had been done before" still represented a considerable gain and should not be underestimated (449; see 425).

Clearly, people commonly believe that they can and need to make moral judgments and that they are obligated to do the morally right thing. Kant had enormous respect for the moral judgments of ordinary people (see, e.g., 404). Had such people been his main reading audience, he could have been content simply to offer a clear analysis of the nature of human morality.

Not everyone, however, agreed that his analysis was correct. The two claims most often attacked were (1) his contention that we can know what morality requires of us without being told by some authority or other and (2) his further claim that we are able to do what morality requires without being motivated by desire, whether a desire for what promises satisfaction of one kind or another or an aversion to an unwanted outcome, such as punishment for wrongdoing. Hume, for example, had held that reason has only the function of serving our desires; and what was even more critical to Kant's political and moral analyses, Hobbes had argued that all rational conduct is motivated by self-interest, by hypothetical policies for satisfying our desires.[1] Moreover, the new Newtonian science regarded the world, of which human beings are a part, as completely governed by inexorable causal laws. In a causally determined world, there is no room for moral ideals about the way things ought to be; everything simply is the way it is. Kant, therefore, felt it essential to defend the claim that we actually are the kind of agents he had held that we are.

THE DEFENSE OF FREEDOM

Kant needed to defend his fundamental claim that, even if we cannot help but be affected by our desires, we still are able to choose and to act independently of them on the basis of our reason. We saw in Chapter 7 that he held that if we are free in that negative sense, we are also free in the positive sense that we have the power to judge autonomously, by a law given only by our own reason – the Law of Autonomy. Moreover, we are able to act on our judgments, relying only on motivation also supplied by our own reason (446–7, 461). Therefore, to defend his analysis of our agency, Kant was forced to justify our right to believe that we really are free and therefore both able to obey the moral law and obligated to do so (447–8). It was to that task that Kant turned in the third section of the *Foundations* (429n).

The defense of our moral agency, he wrote, requires us to answer the question, How is the imperative of morality possible? (419). He restated the same question in other, equivalent ways: How can the moral law be binding? How is a categorical imperative possible? (420, 461). Answering these questions poses special difficulties because the Categorical Imperative is a synthetic a priori practical proposition (420). So there is this further question: How is a synthetic a priori proposition like that possible? (444).

161

To understand this last question, we need to review briefly some of the materials provided as background information in Chapter 2.[2] There we saw that Kant held that propositions or judgments can be either analytic or synthetic. In analytic judgments, the predicate only repeats, perhaps in a partial but more explicit fashion, what is already contained in the meaning of the subject-concept. If an analytic judgment is true, it is necessarily true, or, in more contemporary terms, true by definition. By contrast, in synthetic judgments the predicate is ampliative; that is, it adds new information about the subject.

Kant held that the Law of Autonomy – that an absolutely good agent is one who acts autonomously – is analytically true, for the predicate only makes explicit our ordinary notion of the subject (see 440).[3] Moreover, given the way in which he had defined the terms "free," "moral," and "autonomous," the following claim is also analytically true: if and only if human agents are free can they act autonomously and be bound by moral constraints (447). So Kant described being autonomous, being under the moral law, and being free in the positive sense as "reciprocal" or equivalent concepts: to be one is also to be the others as well (450).

Since, however, we are purportedly moral agents who act on the Law of Autonomy only contingently, that law appears to us as an imperative, as the Categorical Imperative, obligating us never to act contrary to it (449). If we restate that imperative as a *principle* applying to us, it reads: human agents ought to be agents who never disobey the Law of Autonomy. The predicate (agents who never disobey the Law of Autonomy) expresses more than what is denoted by the subject, human agents (who supposedly can obey that law but need not do so). Therefore, the principle is synthetic, joining two distinct ideas, but doing so in an a priori fashion, that is, with necessity, with an "ought" (420, 454).

THE FUTILITY OF AN APPEAL TO EXPERIENCE

Given Kant's description of the Categorical Imperative as a "synthetic a priori practical proposition," the questions he originally asked can now be paraphrased as, How can the categorical "ought" in that imperative be justified? or How can our consciousness of being bound absolutely by moral requirements be confirmed? The answer, again, is that we must be able to defend the claim that we are free. Only if we are free can the moral law bind us in the form of a categorical imperative.

In the case of many synthetic judgments, what justifies our connecting two different concepts is ordinary experience. To say, for example, "The national government is located in Washington, D.C.," is to make a synthetic claim about a relation between two distinct entities. This claim can be verified in an a posteriori fashion, that is, on the basis of experience, but it is only a contingent claim. The national government has not always been located in Washington, D.C., and however unlikely, it could be relocated again. So that claim lacks the necessity found in judgments that hold in an a priori manner. Kant concluded that although experience can verify contingent claims, it can never account for necessary claims such as the Categorical Imperative. They can be demonstrated only by reason, that is, in what Kant called an a priori fashion (420, 448).

In Chapter 7 we discussed Kant's arguments in the first two sections of the *Foundations* against appealing to experience to support an analysis of morality and why in fact it would be devastating to that analysis to insist on doing so (406–12, 419, 427). Now in the third section, he again attacked experience, this time as the support for our freedom.

As we have seen, in Kant's analysis, autonomy is uncaused causality and complete self-determination, and a categorical imperative is an imperative that commands us to act com-

163

pletely independently of *all* prior and present empirical conditions. But in order to have any experience at all, that is, any coherent knowledge and understanding of the world, we must *presuppose* that *everything* happens according to universal causal laws; nothing in our experience can be free of all prior determination (459). As a consequence, it is impossible in principle to locate freedom in the world of experience (447, 459). As far as science is concerned, the concept of a free, moral agency is "empty"; it does not and cannot have any referents in the world. Therefore, there can be no scientific basis for asserting that we have pure reason that can be practical of itself, or for an imperative ordering agents to act freely and spontaneously, on the basis only of their own reasoning. We have no scientific way to prove we are free (448n). For that reason, Kant called the concept of moral freedom "transcendental"; it can refer only to reality that "transcends" the world of experience (452, 455).

Kant allowed that we do feel we are free and therefore obligated by the moral law (447). But the sheer fact that we *feel* free does not prove that we actually *are* free; that feeling may be only a persistent illusion. Kant himself called attention to this objection, but he thought it could be met, and the argument he eventually offered in fact is based on our moral consciousness (448–9, 453, 457).[4]

KANT'S THESIS

Before actually presenting his argument, however, Kant first described how it would proceed. In the following passage, "Now I say that. . . " means what philosophers today mean when they write, "What I now want to claim is that. . . "

> Now I say that every being that cannot act otherwise than under the Idea of freedom is thereby really free in a practical respect. That is to say, all laws that are inseparably bound with freedom hold for it just as if its will were

proved free in itself by theoretical philosophy. (448; see 461)

In a footnote to that sentence, Kant again summarized his argument that even if our freedom is left without a theoretical or scientific proof, "the laws that would obligate a being who was really free would [still] hold for a being who cannot act except under the Idea of his own freedom" (448n).

Kant's argument began by pointing out that, in our practical self-awareness as agents, we are convinced that we *are* free and morally responsible for what we do. This is not just a presupposition that we happen to make; it is one we all find we *must* believe to be true whenever we deliberate about how to act and whenever we do act. Moreover, it is an assumption we must make not only about ourselves but also about all other rational agents as well (429, 447–9). Arguments against our being free are completely irrelevant to us and can have no effect on us, for we are utterly *unable* to live our lives without presuming that we are free and able to act just on the basis of our own reasoning (454–6). This further implies that we must presume that we and all other such agents are therefore obligated to obey the Law of Autonomy (449). Even "the most hardened scoundrel" cannot avoid the conviction that he is morally free and could and should be a better person than he is (454–5).

Before going further, Kant interjected a warning against our trying to *understand* how these convictions can be true, that is, how it is possible for us to be moral agents (450). He did so rather mysteriously, cautioning that such an effort would explain nothing because it would involve "a kind of circle, from which, as it seems, there is no way of escape."

If we try to explain how we can be free, we can do so only by invoking a causal explanation, and if we do that, we end up with a self-contradictory and incoherent claim: human agents are autonomous because they are "freely determined" according to causal laws by prior events not now under those agents' control (450). Alternatively, if we try using a conceptual argument to the effect that freedom is the *cause* of our being autonomous and under the moral law, we only beg the question and explain nothing (453), because Kant had already defined a free will and an autonomous will as "reciprocal," or equivalent, concepts (447, 450). So neither concept can be used to *explain* the other in the sense of accounting for it or being its cause.

Because we cannot explain how it is possible for us to be moral agents, Kant came to two conclusions: first, that "nothing is left but *defense*," that is, the defense of our right to *take* ourselves to be free (459), and, second, that we have no alternative but to look for that defense in our own moral experience, in our own inner rational awareness of our spontaneity when we think practically. His strategy was to introduce his now famous "two-viewpoints" doctrine, which showed, he claimed, that taking ourselves as free and morally obligated is both unavoidable and allowable (450).

THE DOCTRINE OF THE TWO VIEWPOINTS

As we have just seen, for our theoretical purposes, in order to understand the world (and ourselves as part of it), we must regard it as governed by laws of natural necessity; but for practical purposes, for purposes of acting, we also must regard ourselves as free. Moreover, we cannot abandon either view (456).[5] Taking these two standpoints would involve us in a contradiction, Kant wrote, if we were to claim that we are both free and determined in the same respect or the same sense, that is, as beings in the world of sense experience (456, 459).

His solution was to maintain that, although there is only one world, we must regard it from *different viewpoints* when we think for theoretical or for practical purposes (452, 456–8). He had introduced the two-viewpoints doctrine in his earlier *Critique of Pure Reason* as the only way in which we can avoid contradicting ourselves. There he had pointed out that we can *reflect about* how we must take both of these two viewpoints, but we can only *take* one viewpoint at a time, and from each viewpoint we regard the world differently for our different purposes. That, he held, is enough to keep us from contradicting ourselves.

In the third section of the *Foundations,* Kant maintained that, not just philosophers, but persons of "the most ordinary intelligence," take these two standpoints (450). If they are reflective at all, they all realize, at least in a "rough" way, that the world we know through our senses, through experience, consists of reality-as-it-appears-to-us, or what he called the "sensible" or "phenomenal" world (452, 454). All our knowledge of the world is radically dependent on the ways in which our senses and our mental faculties structure the world that we experience. As a result, what we may claim to *know* theoretically or scientifically about reality is *limited* to *appearances.*

Once we become aware of how radically our own perceptual and mental operations affect the way we know the world, Kant wrote, we find it is rationally necessary to assume that appearances do not exhaust reality. There must be something that is not appearance but the ground or cause of the world that appears to us (451). We cannot claim any knowledge of that "something," since we can know only what appears to us in our sensory experience, but we still can and must *think* of reality-as-it-is-in-itself (Kant's famous *Ding an sich*), apart from all the contributions that we make. He called this the "noumenal" or "intelligible" (thinkable) world (450–2).

When we discussed the notion of character in Chapter 8, we saw we also cannot avoid taking these two viewpoints of ourselves (451–3, 456–9). When we think about ourselves theoretically, trying to understand how we affect and are affected by the phenomenal world, we have to regard ourselves as under laws of causal determinism like everything else in that world. But to reason practically, about how to act, we find ourselves involuntarily "constrained" to think of the self that is the ground of our appearance in the phenomenal world. That is, we find we then must regard ourselves as members of the noumenal world – as free from all causal determination and so as autonomous beings bound only by the moral law (453, 458).

We likewise must regard our actions in the world from the same two viewpoints. From the theoretical standpoint, we consider them as events causally conditioned by other appearances, namely, our desires and inclinations. But from the moral viewpoint, we regard them as appearances in the world of our noumenal self, of both our underlying moral disposition and our individual decisions, as their ground or efficient cause.[6]

To conceive of ourselves this way, Kant wrote, "would not be possible" if we were causally determined (458). If we *were* determined by what Kant called "the influences of sensibility," we could just wait passively for our desires and inclinations to determine how we were going to act. If the outcome were already determined, there would be no point in deliberating, except perhaps to figure out how to get what we become aware that we most want. But it does not work that way, not even for a person convinced of determinism. If we just wait, we may become more aware of the various desires we happen to have, but no "decisions" occur. We are not compelled to act on the desires we have, even on one that may seem stronger than the others, for we need not count the satisfaction of any particular desire as being a "good reason" for acting. So we *must* take the point of view that we somehow stand outside the chain of causal connections. We can and therefore must deliberate and choose only on the basis of what we *count* as a good reason for acting.

We are now ready to examine the second part of Kant's thesis: The same laws that "would obligate a being who was really free," that is, for whom we could provide a theoretical proof of its freedom, in fact do obligate a being who cannot act except under the presumption of being free (448n). Kant's claim is that our very ability to exercise spontaneity by thinking of ourselves as members of the noumenal world (and, more strongly, the *necessity* that we do so) is equivalent in cogency, for all *practical* purposes, to the strength of a theoretical proof of our being such members, if such a proof were possible. It then follows that we have the right to *think of ourselves* as free, moral agents, which is *all* that it can mean, within the Kantian system, to say that we really are such agents.

It is important to add that we also must take the point of view that we are free when we think theoretically, so as not to deny that we really are thinking (447–9, 452–3, 457–9). Those of us who are scientists must deliberate about what experiments to do and then make decisions on the basis of that deliberation; and throughout, we clearly are presupposing that we are being led by our own thinking. But because science must rely on information gained through the senses to show what is real, we are placed in an embarrassing position: it *is* clearly in our interest just as thinking beings that our belief in our freedom be defensible, but we cannot provide any scientific evidence to support our freedom. It is important, however, to add that there is also no evidence *against* the possibility of our freedom. In effect, science leaves a space open for the reality of that possibility.

What this means is that any defense of our freedom can be made only from a *practical* point of view. The fact that we all necessarily presume we are free moral agents, Kant argued, gives us a *practical* entitlement to *take* ourselves to be free and subject to the Law of Autonomy. That entitlement is just as strong as if we could claim to know we are free theoretically, on the basis of empirical evidence.

But why should the presumption of freedom from a practical point of view have any more strength than that same presumption from a theoretical point of view? In 452 Kant briefly referred to his theory of knowledge. In order to focus on the issue at hand, we shall attend only to his point in doing so: Our ability to reason – and to reason morally – enjoys more freedom than our ability to understand the world. We can only understand objects in the world theoretically that we can encounter through our sense experience; by contrast, our moral reason can *cause* its own objects (free actions). Since science cannot disprove the possibility of our having such causal power, we have the right to regard ourselves from a moral point of view (i.e., for the purposes of practice) as free and therefore moral agents.

How, in Kant's view, does the doctrine of the two viewpoints keep us from falling into the circularity he had warned against? "When we think of ourselves as free," Kant wrote by way of an explanation, "we transport ourselves into the intelligible world as members of it and know the autonomy of the will together with its consequence, morality" (453). There is no consensus among commentators about what he meant to say here. It may be helpful, however, to discuss his doctrine of the two viewpoints in more detail.

In our initially philosophically naive thinking, we may believe that the world *presents* itself to us as causally structured, but Hume's writings had led Kant to realize that we never actually *see* any causal power. Instead, thinking of the events in the world as bound by causal connections is a point of view *we* project on the world. From this it follows that the way we regard the world theoretically is only *a viewpoint* we take, but one that we find we must take in order to understand the world. Moreover, it is so strongly confirmed by our experience that it would be senseless to try to place it in doubt.

Since all the "conditions of sensibility," including the category of causal connections, originate with *us*, with our understanding and not with the world apart from us, we may and must think of the noumenal world, negatively, as free of the causal laws we project on the world of appearances (451–2,

457–8, 461–2). Nonetheless, we still can and must *think* of our noumenal causality as, like all causes, being under *some* law or other determining its nature *as* a cause. If, from the noumenal point of view, we are independent of all the causal laws of the phenomenal world of sense experience, we must be under the only causal law possible in a free world: We must be a law unto ourselves, under the self-imposed Law of Autonomy.

Taking the noumenal point of view, however, also means that we have no hope of answering any of the "metaphysical" questions Kant initially had posed. That point of view does not and cannot give us any new *theoretical* knowledge of reality, for example, *that* we are free; nor does it function as an *explanation*, helping us understand *how* we are free. Although we may be tempted to ask all sorts of questions about how the noumenal realm operates, it is futile to do so. We simply *cannot* comprehend how we can be free, how pure reason can be practical, how the Categorical Imperative is possible, or how a noumenal efficient cause can manifest itself in the world, whether in moral interest, moral emotions, or actions, without interfering with the causal laws of the phenomenal world. We can only "comprehend [the] incomprehensibility" of our moral agency (463).

Perhaps this discussion can help us better understand how the doctrine of the two viewpoints prevents us from falling into a circular argument. That circularity would consist in trying to appeal to the causal power of our moral reason as an *explanation* of how we can act freely. Such an "explanation" would clearly beg the issue and explain nothing. However, it should now be clear that we have given up trying to use a causal argument to explain our moral agency. We cannot understand *how* we can be free, but for our practical purposes, we do not need to understand our freedom. Moreover, the two-viewpoints doctrine Kant offered in the third section of the *Foundations* has successfully defended our *right to view ourselves as free*, as having the power of pure practical reason, as being moral agents, and therefore as bound by the Law of Autonomy and obligated never to violate it in our actions.

We may have begun this inquiry believing it to be theoretical in nature since it is about what is the case, but in the course of that examination, we found we must give up trying to understand our freedom and focus instead on a defense of our ability and obligation to act morally (462). Kant had enormous sympathy for our rational interest in wanting to understand how we can be free and how the Categorical Imperative is possible, but as he wrote, we at least now know what we need to know for the sake of moral practice, and that "is all that can fairly be demanded of a philosophy which in its principles strives to reach to the boundary of human reason" (463).

A SECOND ARGUMENT

After publication of the *Foundations,* Kant continued to reflect on his defense of our right to believe in our own freedom and moral agency, and three years later, in his *Critique of Practical Reason,* he argued that we *can* go beyond a defense because we have positive and indubitable support for our belief. Having established to his own satisfaction the legitimacy of appealing, for the sake of practice, to our own moral self-consciousness, he held we become aware of the moral law "as a fact of reason" within the spontaneous activity of our practical reason. We experience ourselves as bound by that law when, in the middle of the familiar internal moral conflicts we all have, it commands our obedience in opposition to all our desires and inclinations. It thereby reveals its reality to us in the form of the Categorical Imperative.

By a "fact" Kant meant either an object whose reality can be proved or a concept that is valid in the sense that there really is something that it denotes. We prove the reality of empirical facts from experience; and we learn of this moral fact a priori by its appearance in our reason, that is, in our moral awareness. The Categorical Imperative, he wrote, is "the sole fact of pure reason," because it is the only law that practical reason can give to itself. It is not possible for us to have a direct apprehension of the ultimate moral norm itself, since it is the law of supersensuous nature. Rather, we become aware of its constraining effect on our thinking. Since it is thereby "firmly established by itself," we now know that the moral law is no longer in need of a defense. The "moral fact" of its impact on our moral consciousness shows that "pure reason is practical of itself alone" and that we are moral agents.

The practical "fact" of the moral law, Kant wrote, is also sufficient ground for us to infer that we are free. He continued to hold that freedom is the ground of the possibility of the moral law, but he now believed that "the moral law is the only condition under which freedom can be *known*." That law commands us to master our desires and inclinations, and because it is our own reason that gives us that law, we can infer that we can do what it commands. The reality of our freedom is just as certain as that of the moral law itself, even though we cannot understand *how* we can be free. From the point of view of theoretical knowledge, then, our freedom remains only a subjective postulate, and our belief in our freedom a faith. But from the point of view of moral reasoning, our freedom is an objectively valid Idea; it is as undeniable as anything we can know theoretically.

NOTES

1. Kant's contention that the state needs to enact sanctions for law-breakers only reflected his conviction that not everyone will do what is right *despite* their moral ability to do so.
2. See note 5 in Chapter 2.
3. In 447 Kant seemed to claim that the principle of morality, which he had already said he had derived *analytically* from the concept of a good will (445), is a *synthetic* proposition. What he apparently

meant was that that principle appears *to us* as a synthetic a priori principle, since we are only contingently moral.

4. Kant called this kind of argument a (transcendental) deduction; it consists in asking what conditions *must* hold true in order that the "given" (here the freedom that we all suppose we have) may be possible, even if not completely explained or understood. Kant's argument in the *Foundations* bears some similarity to the "demonstration by way of refutation" that Aristotle had used in Book Gamma of his *Metaphysics*. Aristotle had wanted to defend the principle of noncontradiction from attacks by radical skepticism. But that principle is so fundamental that it cannot be inferred from any prior truths. So, rather than try to provide some sort of positive proof – an impossible task – Aristotle undertook only to *defend* that principle, by pointing out that any attack on it presupposes it as a tacit premise and is therefore self-defeating. In a similar way Kant wanted to defend a viewpoint so fundamental it cannot be based on anything else and also is presupposed even by attacks on it.

5. Exactly why our minds work this way, Kant wrote, is a further question so absolutely fundamental that we can have no insight into it (463).

6. The actions we see are always only "clues" to a person's moral character, and our judgments are always based only on inferences, rather than certainties. "When moral value is in question, it is a matter not of actions one sees but of their inner principles, which one does not see" (407). We can never be *certain* that any action, even an action of our own, has been done with the right moral intention (406–8).

SUGGESTIONS FOR
FURTHER READING

From the very beginning, Kant's ideas engendered an enormous secondary literature as well as differing interpretations of those ideas. Readers of this book may therefore be interested in other authors who present parts of Kant's ethics in greater detail or whose interpretations may differ from those offered herein. The collection below includes works that seem particularly appropriate for this book's readers.

Secondary literature cannot substitute for Kant's own writings. Mention should therefore be made of the first comprehensive edition of the works of Kant in English translation, begun in 1992 by Cambridge University Press, which will continue until completed in fourteen volumes.

Acton, H. B. *Kant's Moral Philosophy*. New York: St. Martin's Press, 1970. This work is widely acknowledged as a fine brief introduction to Kant's ethics.

Beck, Lewis White. *A Commentary on Kant's Critique of Practical Reason*. Chicago: University of Chicago Press, 1960. Most people writing about Kant today were reared on this author's translations, books, and articles. Although written over thirty years ago, this book, which also covers all the principal parts of the *Foundations*, is still the standard commentary on Kant's *Critique of Practical Reason*. Also recommended is a volume of essays by the same author: *Studies in the Philosophy of Kant* (Indianapolis: Bobbs-Merrill, 1965).

Gregor, Mary J. *Laws of Freedom*. New York: Barnes & Noble, 1963. This is the only detailed commentary on the *Metaphysics of Morals*, a book in which Kant applied the Categorical Imperative to both public and personal life. Although now out of print, copies of this book should be available in most college and university libraries.

Guyer, Paul, ed. *The Cambridge Companion to Kant.* Cambridge: Cambridge University Press, 1992. This collection of essays on Kant's theoretical and practical philosophy is written for both advanced students and professional philosophers. Especially recommended are J. B. Schneewind's "Autonomy, Obligation, and Virtue: An Overview of Kant's Moral Philosophy" and Allen W. Wood's "Rational Theology, Moral Faith, and Religion."

Herman, Barbara. *The Practice of Moral Judgment.* Cambridge, Mass.: Harvard University Press, 1993. This collection of essays by a leading interpreter of Kant's ethics focuses on the role of moral judgment as well as on the nature of moral personality in Kant's theory.

Hill, Thomas E., Jr. *Autonomy and Self-Respect.* Cambridge: Cambridge University Press, 1991. The essays in this volume model the way in which one might explore specific moral problems and moral attitudes from a Kantian, rather than consequentialist, perspective. Because they articulate the issues so clearly, these articles are often anthologized.

Hill, Thomas E., Jr. *Dignity and Practical Reason in Kant's Moral Theory.* Ithaca, N.Y.: Cornell University Press, 1992. The introduction to this volume offers a nice overview of the *Foundations,* followed by chapters focusing on many of the major themes both in that book and in the *Metaphysics of Morals.*

Kosgaard, Christine M. "Kant's Formula of Universal Law," *Pacific Philosophical Quarterly* 66 (1985): 24–47; "Kant's Formula of Humanity," *Kant-Studien* 77 (1986): 183–202; "Two Distinctions in Goodness," *Philosophical Review* 92 (1983): 169–95. These are only some of the essays by this author soon to be gathered into a collection by Cambridge University Press. They are often cited by others writing on Kant's ethics.

Michalson, Gordon E., Jr. *Fallen Freedom: Kant on Radical Evil and Moral Regeneration.* Cambridge: Cambridge University Press, 1990. This book analyzes part of the background of Kant's view of human nature and includes a helpful bibliography.

O'Neill, Onora. *Constructions of Reason: Explorations of Kant's Practical Philosophy.* Cambridge: Cambridge University Press, 1990. The author, a distinguished philosopher, argues that Kant's views about freedom and moral agency are only part of his larger critique of reason. The author also pays particular attention to the analysis of maxims as principles of obligation.

Paton, H. J. *The Categorical Imperative: A Study in Kant's Moral Philosophy.* Philadelphia: University of Pennsylvania Press, (1947) 1971. This often reprinted commentary on the *Foundations* has been described as the "best sympathetic interpretation of Kant's ethical theory." Although now somewhat dated, its scholarship is solid, and the book is still often cited today.

Rawls, John. *A Theory of Justice.* Cambridge, Mass.: Harvard University Press, 1971. This book has been described as "the most substantial contribution to moral philosophy written in English since World War II." Because this study is an extension of Kant's contractarian political philosophy, its publication was influential in generating a renewed interest in Kant's ethics.

Rawls, John. *Political Liberalism.* New York: Columbia University Press, 1993. In this volume the author further develops the concept of a stable and just society for citizens holding different and deeply conflicting religious, philosophical, and moral doctrines.

Sullivan, Roger J. *Immanuel Kant's Moral Theory.* Cambridge: Cambridge University Press, 1989. This comprehensive study of Kant's ethics is, on the whole, accessible to students as well as philosophers, emphasizing differing interpretations in voluminous footnotes; it includes an extensive bibliography.

Williams, Howard Lloyd, ed. *Essays on Kant's Political Philosophy.* Chicago: University of Chicago Press, 1992. Historical events in the twentieth century have offered striking new support for the validity of Kant's political and moral thought, justifying renewed attention to his views, as shown by this recent collection of essays.

Wood, Allen W. *Kant's Moral Religion.* Ithaca, N.Y.: Cornell University Press, 1970. The author is the leading expert in the United States on Kant's theological and religious writings and beliefs, as well as their influence on his moral thought.

INDEX

NATIONAL UNIVERSITY
LIBRARY   SAN DIEGO

NATIONAL UNIVERSITY
LIBRARY   SAN DIEGO

.4790